HITLER'S WAR MACHINE

PANZERS AT WAR
1943-1945

BOB CARRUTHERS

Pen & Sword
MILITARY

This edition published in 2013 by
Pen & Sword Military
An imprint of
Pen & Sword Books Ltd
47 Church Street
Barnsley
South Yorkshire
S70 2AS

First published in Great Britain in 2011 in digital format by
Coda Books Ltd.

Copyright © Coda Books Ltd, 2011
Published under licence by Pen & Sword Books Ltd.

ISBN 978 1 78159 131 4

The moral right of Bob Carruthers to be identified as the author of this work has been asserted in
accordance with the Copyright, Designs and Patents Act, 1988.

A CIP catalogue record for this book is
available from the British Library

Printed and bound by CPI Group (UK) Ltd, Croydon, CR0 4YY

Pen & Sword Books Ltd incorporates the Imprints of Pen & Sword Aviation, Pen & Sword Family
History, Pen & Sword Maritime, Pen & Sword Military, Pen & Sword Discovery, Pen & Sword
Politics, Pen & Sword Atlas, Pen & Sword Archaeology, Wharncliffe Local History, Wharncliffe
True Crime, Wharncliffe Transport, Pen & Sword Select, Pen & Sword Military Classics, Leo
Cooper, The Praetorian Press, Claymore Press, Remember When, Seaforth Publishing and Frontline
Publishing

For a complete list of Pen & Sword titles please contact
PEN & SWORD BOOKS LIMITED
47 Church Street, Barnsley, South Yorkshire, S70 2AS, England
E-mail: enquiries@pen-and-sword.co.uk
Website: www.pen-and-sword.co.uk

CONTENTS

HIGH NOON AT KURSK 4

PANZERKAMPFWAGEN V SD.KFZ.171 40

ACTION IN ITALY AND NORMANDY 45

OPERATIONAL STATUS OF TIGERS ON THE
EASTERN AND WESTERN FRONTS..................................67

PANZERKAMPFWAGEN VI (B)SD.KFZ. 182....................68

TANK NUMBERING...71

THE WESTERN FRONT 1944 - 1945 72

LAST BATTLES IN THE EAST...92

APPENDIX 112

MORE FROM THE SAME SERIES..................................123

HIGH NOON AT KURSK

"As we passed the unfamiliar column of Panzers, it was soon obvious that there had been a serious problem with one machine in particular that was reduced to a burnt out wreck with no sign of any enemy activity. We later learnt that this was the Panther – Guderian's problem child!"

SS PANZER GRENADIER HOFSTETTER, ON KURSK

A rare shot of the Tiger from the pages of Signal magazine.

Under peacetime conditions, normally, a new fighting vehicle would be designed, built and tested over a period of something like five years. Between 1941 and 1945 some very successful designs were produced in as many months. They had to be. The war in the East was a demanding and remorseless taskmaster which consumed every new offering as soon as it was ready for action. The price of failure was unthinkable.

From 1943 onwards, German engineers were driven by the desperate demands of a voracious front line which threatened to consume their very homeland if they did not supply exactly the right technology.

Despite the vile excesses of the regime under which they toiled, German factories produced an outstanding variety of armoured fighting vehicles in an incredibly short period of time. It has often been said that the German armaments industry placed the best possible weapons in the worst possible hands; that is certainly true of the armoured fighting vehicles.

Obviously, there were many failures, but against heavy odds, there were also a large number of successful vehicle types which shaped the face of armoured warfare for years to come.

SELF-PROPELLED ARTILLERY

One successful new breed, created in response to the demands of the Russian front, were the self-propelled artillery vehicles which were rushed into production from the war-ravaged German factories to shore up the defensive battles of that terrible conflict. Mobile artillery on fully-tracked chassis had been proposed as early as 1936 by Heinz Guderian, who for a long time harboured a grudge over its rejection. Now with the Panzer Divisions deployed in the role of a mobile fire brigade which could be rushed from place to place on the crumbling front, mobile artillery was to supply the needs of a military situation which was declining on an almost daily basis.

By 1942 the use of tracked vehicles to support the objectives of the Wehrmacht had grown exponentially. The Army of 1942 was much more mobile, Panzer Grenadiers moving swiftly around the battlefield in armoured half tracks which had gone from 60 in service in Poland to 6,000 in service in Russia. But even mobile infantry still required equally mobile artillery support to achieve many of their objectives.

The Sturmgeschütz assault gun had originally been designed to provide this support, but by 1942 battlefield necessities meant that they were often hijacked into the role of tank destroyers. This left a gap which could not be filled by conventional medium or heavy artillery, these heavier guns often lagging behind the motorised troops across the huge distances which had to

This photograph is part of a sequence which originally appeared in Signal magazine in February 1943, showing the construction of an assembly line to make Marder tank destroyers. The haste with which the plant had to be designed and built mirrors the speed with which the Marder had to be completed and thrown into action, despite its less than satisfactory design.

be covered in Russia.

In Europe, during the campaigns of 1939-1941, where roads were good it was found that conventional artillery could be moved and deployed reasonably easily. But in Russia the dirt roads turned to rivers of mud with the arrival of spring and autumn rains, and they were frequently covered in deep snow during the winter months.

It was now belatedly recognised that Guderian had been correct, and the best possible solution was the deployment of large calibre self-propelled guns on fully tracked carriages. These vehicles could stick reasonably close to the fast-moving Panzer Divisions, and provide them with the same heavy artillery support which would normally require horse-drawn or motorised transport.

Ultimately, thousands of self-propelled guns in a bewildering variety of variations would be employed.

Although it was the insistent demands of the Russian front which provided the real catalyst for the development of self propelled guns, there were a number of earlier precedents. Limited numbers of self-propelled guns called Schwere Infanterie Geschütz, or SIG for short, had been successfully deployed in the 1940 campaign in France.

Initially, these vehicles used the ridiculously light Panzer I chassis to carry the heavy 15cm infantry gun. The troops advanced using the gun to blast infantry from buildings and strong points, and despite the obvious limitations of these first self-propelled guns, the High Command was now aware that there was an increased role for them.

The Germans have long been famous for the quality of their engineering work. They are also justifiably renowned for their meticulousness. A demonstration of this can be seen in the thorough manner in which every tank chassis manufactured during the Second World War was methodically exploited, with uniform thoroughness and regularity, to produce a wide array of specialist vehicles to cater for every need on the battlefield.

Each of the tank chassis produced by German manufacturers or by her Czechoslovakian satellite suppliers, was systematically altered to produce, not just the main battle tanks themselves, but in almost every case, a tank destroyer variant, and a self-propelled artillery variant. There were also command tanks, anti-aircraft tanks, armoured ammunition carriers, armoured recovery vehicles and even flame-throwing tanks.

In the case of self-propelled artillery, this systematic approach to the design possibilities of each model was first seen in the Panzer I, Germany's first and smallest tank. It had proved to be hopelessly inadequate under combat conditions. The armour was too thin and the two-machine-gun armament was ineffective, but the chassis itself was a good one and German engineers immediately set to work to produce specialist variants for other battlefield tasks.

It was the successful adaptation of the Panzer I chassis which allowed the Sig 33 to carry a heavy 15cm gun, to give a heavy self propelled artillery piece which could be moved right up to the front line.

However, there was one major drawback in that the arrangement of such a big gun on such a small chassis: it was so top-heavy that the gun was very liable to tilt over. This undignified trait led to the search for a better alternative. Naturally, the first step was to examine the larger chassis of the other German light tank in service, the Panzer II.

Like the Panzer I, the Panzer II battle tank was found to be woefully inadequate under combat conditions, and, like the Panzer I, an extended Panzer II chassis was successfully developed as a 15cm self-propelled gun carriage in an attempt to extend the life of the design.

In this respect, the Panzer II worked only a little better than the Panzer I. Although it gave a slightly lower profile, and hence better stability and a greater measure of protection to the crew, it was only manufactured in tiny quantities. Only 12 were made and all appear to have been despatched to Africa to equip the Afrika Korps.

In practice, neither the Panzer I or the Panzer II chassis could really deal with the requirement of the heavy 15cm gun which they were being adapted to carry. The lateral solution to the problem was found by reducing the weight of the gun. This produced the Wespe (or Wasp) which combined the lighter 10.5cm gun on a Panzer II chassis. The Wespe was an excellent design, light enough to keep up with the troops, but heavy enough to produce an effective barrage. 682 of these machines were produced from 1942 to 1944. They were welcomed with open arms by the hard-pressed men in the front lines. One thing which did not find favour was the name; it did not suggest power and presence, and was dropped on the personal orders of Hitler in 1944. However, they continued to be known as Wasps to the troops, who did value their considerable sting in battle.

With the introduction of the Wespe, the possibilities for the Panzer II chassis appeared to have been exhausted. The Russian front required heavier guns, so German engineers moved on to examine the possibilities inherent in the Panzer III, which was Germany's main battle tank in the early years of the war. This proved to be a much more fertile hunting ground.

The main variant produced using the Panzer III chassis was, of course, the famous Sturmgeschütz.

To supplement the assault guns it was now obvious that the Wehrmacht needed a purpose-designed vehicle capable of heavier artillery support.

The solution was to adapt the Panzer IV chassis to produce the Hummel or 'Bumble Bee'. The Hummel carried a heavy 15cm gun for mobile artillery bombardment. This vehicle overcame all of the drawbacks of the previous self-propelled guns: it carried a much heavier punch, could be very rapidly deployed and, of course, it could be easily moved to avoid counter-barrages by enemy guns. 666 machines eventually entered service there was a huge demand from the front line units and there were never enough to go round.

The Hummel and the Wespe were to prove highly successful under battlefield conditions. Both could give mobile artillery support to the hard-pressed Panzer Divisions then quickly move location.

In total, some 1,300 of these two types of self-propelled guns were made from 1942 to 1945, during which time they provided essential artillery support to the great advances of 1942 and covering fire for the desperate Wehrmacht Divisions during their headlong retreat back into Germany during 1944.

The only major drawback of these self-propelled guns was the lack of storage space for stocks of ammunition. In the case of the Hummel there was only enough room for 18 rounds. Constant re-supplying was therefore required during any significant bombardments.

However, by 1944 ammunition supplies were strictly limited in the German forces and, unlike the glory days of 1941, even these limited stocks had to be shepherded very carefully indeed.

In line with the German factories, the tank-producing Skoda works in Czechoslovakia also produced self-propelled artillery using the chassis from the Czech manufactured tanks. The Czech-made Panzer 38(t) equipped many German units during the early years of the war, and when the tanks were withdrawn from front line service in 1942 it made sense to convert the highly serviceable chassis into a self-propelled artillery role.

The resultant machine, which combined a 10.5cm howitzer with the 38(t) chassis, was known to the Germans as the 'Grille', or Cricket. In post-war years a number of authorities have suggested it was also known to the troops as 'the Bison', although the sources for this are uncertain. No action reports refer to these vehicles by any other name than Crickets. They were never as popular as the Wespe or the Hummel: nevertheless, 282 machines were manufactured and they saw action mainly in Russia. A few were also used in the campaign in the west after the Allied landings.

Unlike the Panzer I, II and III, the Panzer IV remained in service throughout the war, so there was never likely to be a surplus of redundant vehicles for conversion. In any case, the successful introduction of the Wespe and Hummel solved the technical problems of mobile heavy artillery support. In consequence, further attempts to use the Panzer IV chassis for self-propelled artillery were limited to a few experiments which produced a machine nicknamed the Grasshopper. This is a very rare machine indeed, of which only a few were produced. Some sources put the figure as low as two machines, others say 14 were made. With the warped logic which led to its creation, that's no great surprise.

In order to allow for the turret to give the protection the crew needed, the gun size had to be reduced to 10.5cm, when what was actually demanded were heavier calibre guns. But the Panzer IV produced one of the most successful designs in the form of the Panzerjäger IV, a superb tank hunter.

By this stage of the wartime was beginning to run against the Germans, and the Panzer V and VI chassis did not produce as many conversions as previous vehicles.

THE PRELUDE TO KURSK

In the wake of the German disaster at Stalingrad in February 1943, the Red Army continued its lightning advance. Finally the 1st SS Panzer Corps, who were part of Army Group South, managed to halt the Soviet thrust around Kharkov in March 1943. To the north, the hard-pushed Army Group Centre had also managed to stall the Russian advance around the region ol Orel. Together these two German Army Groups were just about managing to hold the Russian attacks. However, between their positions was a huge Russian bulge. The width of the salient was about 100 miles wide and 80 miles deep, centred around the town of Kursk. Hitler ordered that this salient was to be cut off and the Soviet forces inside destroyed.

The plan itself was simple; it called for the inspirational handling of armoured forces. With their proven record of success the men of the German tank corps felt they were equal to the task. The 9th Army would attack from Orel in the north, the 4th Panzer Army would attack from Belgorod in the south. These two great advances would meet in the middle and trap the Russians inside a huge pocket. They could then concentrate on the destruction of these trapped forces. The architect of this great scheme was Field Marshall von Manstein, who was an experienced veteran with a good understanding of armour in battle.

The Russian forces facing the Zitadelle offensive were aware that their forces were vulnerable here.

Both sides could see that this area could represent the decisive battle of the campaign so far. Germany was keen to regain the initiative in Russia after the Stalingrad debacle, and the recent success at Kharkov had provided an important but small taste of what could be achieved. Nonetheless, Hitler did have misgivings about this offensive and he even confessed to Guderian that the thought of it 'made his stomach turn over'. To the troops, however, he stressed the importance of this forthcoming battle. He boasted that the coming victory at Kursk will be a 'beacon for the whole world'. It was a measure of his anxiety that the out-of-favour General Heinz Guderian was recalled to oversee the preparation of the new armoured forces for the battle. This led to the creation of a specialist Tank Ordnance headquarters.

EQUIPMENT AND AMMUNITION ORGANISATION

Previously the same organisation had served the Panzer forces as well as the other formations of the Wehrmacht. The agencies responsible for most of the storage, issue, and repair of equipment and for the storage, issue, and salvaging of ammunition belonged to a separate branch of the Army, the Ordnance Branch (Feldzeugwesen). This branch was headed by the Chief Army Ordnance Officer (Feldzeugmeister), who worked through his staff, the Ordnance Inspectorate (Feldzeuginspektion) in the General Army Office (Allgemeines Heeresamt). From the Ordnance Inspectorate the chain of command led through three regional commands, called Ordnance Groups (Feldzeuggruppen), with headquarters in Berlin, Kassel, and Munich, to the Ordnance Headquarters (Feldzeugkommandos) which were at the level of the corps areas but not affiliated with the latter. There was one Ordnance Headquarters in each corps area, where it controlled a varying number of equipment and ammunition

The difficult logistics of moving tanks by trailer meant that the Panzers were frequently driven long distances on these trailers resulting in a high level of breakdowns.

depots. The Ordnance Headquarters was the lowest controlling agency for the storage and issue of equipment and ammunition, below this level they were handled by two separate types of depots. The Ordnance Headquarters was designated by the number of the corps area. Ordnance Headquarters and the depots it controlled were not, however, part of the corps area organisation.

In addition to the Ordnance Headquarters designated by the corps area numbers, there existed an Ordnance Headquarters, which was in charge of a great number of subterranean ammunition depots in central Germany. In 1943 the special Tank Ordnance Headquarters, (Panzer-Feldzeugkommando), was created. This was done in order to centralise the supply of all types of armoured fighting vehicles and their spare parts throughout the German forces.

FUELS AND LUBRICANTS

The question of fuel supply may seem rather unspectacular but it was the lifeblood of the Panzer Divisions. The system was complex. Fuel from home fuel depots or from field army mobile reserves was directed to the railheads. Sometimes the fuel was kept loaded in tanker trains (Eisenbahntankstellen) near the railhead and transferred from these directly to fuel columns, but preferably it was laid down in 20 and 200-litre containers in Army Fuel Dumps (Armeebetriebesstofflager) forward of the railhead. From these dumps the fuel was taken on to Division Fuel Distributing Points (Divisionbetriebsstoffausgabesstellen) or, in the case of armoured Divisions, to Division Fuel Dumps (Divisionbetriebsstofflager). Fuel was then forwarded from the Division area to lower echelon supply points and to fuel points that were set aside for the use of single vehicles (Tankstellen fur Einzelkraftfahrzeuge). The latter could also be supplied from the Army fuel stores.

Perhaps even more important than the Field Army Motor Transport Parks were the Field Army Tank Parks or Bases (Stutzpunkte). These were established on the basis of one per Army group. Their importance was increased by the fact that Armies did not ordinarily maintain fixed installations for the repair of tanks, although Armies had semi-permanent tank workshops. The tank bases were reception or control centres from which tanks could be dispatched to workshops in the near vicinity for repairs, or returned to home depots and factories for rear echelon maintenance.

SUPPLY REQUIREMENTS

The determination of the overall requirements necessary to maintain a German field Division presented a number of difficulties. This is best shown by a review of the German supply expenditures in Russia in 1941. Armoured Divisions averaged some 30 tons daily when inactive and about 700 tons a day when engaged in heavy fighting; infantry Divisions required 80 tons a day when inactive and 1,100 tons during a day of heavy fighting. When engaged in defensive, mopping-up, or minor offensive activities, the Divisions required supplies in amounts somewhere between the two extremes. By far the most important variable in this campaign was the amount of ammunition expended. Requirements of fuel and equipment also varied considerably particularly among the armoured Divisions, while rations and clothing consumption remained relatively static. Expenditures depended upon the nature of the action involved, the types of units engaged, the zone of action, the season of the year, the amount of material available for consumption, and the facility with which supply movements could be made.

PANZER MAINTENANCE

Minor repairs to armoured vehicles (including tanks, self-propelled weapons and other armoured vehicles) were made by unit mechanics and by mobile tank-workshop units. If the repairs could not be completed in the Division area within three days. the vehicles were sent to semi-permanent Army tank workshops or to Field Army Tank Parks or Bases. When armoured vehicles were so badly damaged that they could not be repaired in the field, they were cannibalised or forwarded to tank equipment depots or factories in the home area. In the latter case the vehicles were no longer under Field Army control and were not returned to the units to which they were originally assigned.

Armoured vehicles were of course repaired on the spot if possible. Otherwise they were moved rearward under their own power. Tank transporters were used only when long movements were contemplated or when vehicles could not move under their own power.

For the coming offensive at Kursk, Hitler knew that he was approaching his last opportunity to win a decisive victory in the East. For that reason he ordered the deployment of some of the latest designs in German tanks, even though some of them had not been properly tested.

One such variant was the Rhinoceros or Nashorn; it carried the 88cm Pak 43, the latest 88mm anti-tank gun, mounted on the hybrid chassis of the Pz. Kpfw. III and IV. The vehicle's silhouette was very high and the armour protection given to the crew by the thin-skinned superstructure was very poor. The gun, however, was able to engage tanks at very long range and was loved by its crews.

HERR SENEBERG

Herr Seneberg was a veteran of the Kursk battle. He was a gun-loader on a Nashorn self-propelled tank-hunter, and sixty years later recalled his experiences in the build-up to Kursk:

"The veterans who marched on Stalingrad said to us, "hopefully we'll get better tanks now." They had marched on Stalingrad and they were still partially equipped with tanks that had the 50mm - the 'door knocker' we called it. We were inferior to the Russians as far as tanks were concerned. They had the legendary T-34, a completely different type of tank weapon.

"Once we had been withdrawn, we were told that we would be getting new tank destroyers with the 88mm – a long-barrelled gun – and that's what happened. We were given new 'tanks,' but as we were anti-tank gunners, we had a long-barrelled 88mm gun on an open carriage. The body of the tank was from a Mark III with our gun on top. Yes, we had armour, but the tank was open on the upper part. A normal tank could swing the turret - we couldn't. We had an action radius of only 45 degrees and the rest was up to the driver who had to direct the tank to the left or the right. With this new anti-tank gun we were more than a match for the Russians- we destroyed over thirty T-34's.

"After we had been trained on the guns we were sent to the area of Orel, Kursk - the Kursk Bend we called it – where a final attempt was to be made by the German army to go on the offensive. To the south of us, in Prokhorovka, was the greatest mass of our tanks ever collected in battle.

"Then it started. We wanted to attack but the Russians intended to do the same thing, and one offensive met the other. The Russians were stronger in material and had a greater number of men. When we advanced on this offensive there came a dreadful barrage. And what was it like for me? The

A study of a column of Sturmgeschütz armed with the long-barrelled 75mm gun moving into action.

worst thing I ever experienced. My father, who had been injured in the First World War at Verdun, told me what that was like. I think this must have been the same. The ground looked as if it had been ploughed up. The barrage ended after three hours and then the fighting began.

"At first our tanks were called 'Nashorner' or 'Rhinoceroses', but so that the Russians would get fooled, the name was later changed to 'Hornisse' or 'Hornets'. After our offensive collapsed we were fighting near Orel. The Russians were superior and we had to retreat further and further. We were then given assistance from a tank called the 'Ferdinand'. The biggest tank shell could hit it - it was practically invulnerable. There were still some left after the Kursk battle. The name came ostensibly from Ferdinand Porsche - that's why it was called the Ferdinand. The earth was practically shaking when the Ferdinand was three kilometres away. I know people say they are no good, but I saw them destroy a number of enemy tanks. However, autumn weather set in and the ground went soggy - the Ferdinand was not prepared for that. The Ferdinands which were left after the big battle got damaged motors and they all broke down.

"Eventually we got a direct hit; it must have penetrated the armour at the front where the driver sat with the radio operator. I sat up at the top as I was a gun-loader, and I fed the shells into the barrel. I remember the tank shook, the tracks burst off and we had to jump out at the back. There were four of us left - the Commander, me and the two others. They trampled on top of me and I fell over and saw them running to the left across a cornfield towards the wood. Then I heard them screaming terribly because they had been caught in the machine-gun fire. I had good luck I ran off to the right and got away."

ENTER THE PANTHER

One vehicle with more than its fair share of teething problems was the new Panzer Mk V, better known as the Panther. With the emergence of the Russian T-34 in the autumn of 1941 the Germans quickly realised that they would have to come up with an effective antidote. The plans for a heavier tank were revisited and work began in earnest. The resultant design produced a 45-ton tank, which was still classed as a 'medium' tank by the Germans.

The Panther had the same sloping armour, wide tracks and a similar 75mm gun. Developed with breakneck speed, and rushed into production, the Panther made its debut at the Battle of Kursk, before it was really proven. Engine and transmission problems abounded. Engine fires were commonplace, dozens broke down and some vehicles went into their first action pouring fire from the exhaust pipes. Not surprisingly, the Panther was a disappointment at Kursk, but once it had overcome its initial teething problems, it would prove itself the best 'medium' of the war.

The Panther was a far better vehicle than the T-34 but it was never to be available in the quantities which the war in the East demanded. Although 6,000 would be built, that was never enough, as the numbers destroyed always kept pace with supply.

The advent of the Panther and the Tiger represented almost the end of the evolutionary trail in the Second World War. German tank sizes had steadily increased, from the 6-ton Panzer I to the 22-ton Panzer III and now onto the 62-ton Tiger. It would reach a peak with the 70-ton Tiger B, or King Tiger. The weight and superior armour certainly made the difference, but the quality had been achieved at the expense of quantity and it was quantity which Germany needed.

THE TIGER IN RUSSIA

The Tiger first saw action near Leningrad in August 1942. The results were poor due to inadequate infantry protection and poor deployment. The Russians were able to knock the tanks out by aiming at the tracks. The Germans quickly learned their lesson and future use of the Tiger I was carefully managed. The first large employment of the tank was at Kursk, when approximately one hundred were used. Almost half of these were issued to the elite formations of the Waffen-SS and the Grossdeutchland Division. The Tiger I quickly earned a fearsome reputation among its enemies. This tank only saw action for two years, but its reputation still endures today.

Unlike the Panther, the Tiger was designed on familiar German lines, but all the dimensions were increased. The main armament was the 8.8cm Kw.K 36, which was essentially the 8.8cm Flak 36 adapted for turret mounting. The mounting of such a heavy gun raised considerable problems of rigidity, and consequently the hull was constructed of large plates entirely welded together. The superstructure was made up in one unit, and welded to the hull. The turret wall was made from a single large piece of armour, 82mm thick, bent into a horseshoe shape. To give further protection all the armour plates were interlocked, in addition to being welded. The armour of the Tiger, at the time of its appearance, was the thickest ever to be fitted on any German tank; the front vertical plate was 102mm thick and the hull sides 62mm.

The suspension, which employed interleaved, Christie-type bogie wheels with a very wide track, was reasonably simple and was an effective solution to the problems of such a large and heavy vehicle.

The Tiger engine required very skilled driving and maintenance to get the best performance, and in the hands of insufficiently trained crews mechanical troubles were apt to appear. This characteristic was the tank's principal disadvantage.

THE TIGER IN ACTION

The five-man crew was the standard for all German medium and heavy tanks. The crew of a Tiger consisted firstly of the commander, who was in charge of the vehicle and selected targets. He also fired the turret machine gun. Next came the gunner, who sat next to the commander and targeted his enemies through his gun sights. In many respects, he was the most vital member of the crew. In battle, every shot had to count. The flight of a shell is affected by many factors, including wind direction, rain, snow and other atmospheric conditions. The gunner had to gauge the range to the target, allow for any climatic factors and compensate for the speed of any moving targets, which were more difficult to hit. One miss could allow an enemy tank to get in the first vital shot, which spelt death in the tense tank duels of the Second World War.

The main 88mm armament of the Tiger was aimed and fired as a result of a team effort. It was the job of all members of the Tiger crew to use their vision devices to identify potential targets and to report them to the commander. The Tiger commander would then prioritise the target and would give orders to engage it. The gunner would traverse the Tiger's turret using a hydraulic system controlled by a foot pedal, aim the gun using a binocular telescope sight and then fire the gun using an electrical ignition system.

The loader was responsible for selecting the correct type of ammunition from the ammunition bins, which were included in the Tiger's structure, and using an automatic or semi-automatic loading system to load the gun.

After each engagement he also had the laborious job of emptying the shell cases and restocking the tank with the cumbersome rounds for the main gun.

Inside the hull, towards the front of the vehicle, sat the driver. On his right was the radio operator, who fulfilled the vital communications function, and also manned the hull machine gun.

The usual practice was for the crew of a tank to paint a white ring around the gun barrel for every enemy tank destroyed. Some crews were so successful that a thick white ring had to be painted, representing ten kills. The most successful commanders proudly carried an array of kill rings like so many strutting peacocks.

WITTMAN AND THE TIGER

During his time away from action, Michael Wittmann was promoted to SS-Untersturmführer. On Christmas Day 1942 he received his transfer to Fallingbostel for the formation of the new heavy tank company. Wittmann once again changed his grey assault gun uniform for a black Panzer uniform.

A Tiger rolls past a group of grenadiers during the build-up to the battle of Kursk. Although the Tigers acquitted themselves well in the battle, poor battlefield reconnaissance resulted in large numbers being lost to minefields, which had not been adequately cleared.

There were rumours of a new miracle weapon which filled Michael Wittmann and his colleagues with anticipation. For once, these rumours were true. The Germans were to be equipped with the mighty Tiger tanks, but there was also disappointment for Wittmann. Each Tiger company had a few of the old Panzer IIIs for scouting and support. As he had experience in armoured cars and had trained using these machines, Wittmann was assigned to a Panzer III.

Wittmann was anxious for a Tiger of his own, but he had a long wait. Finally, in March 1943, he achieved his aim and stood for the first time in the turret of a Tiger, as its commander.

Wittmann could afford no time to reflect on his new status. The strategic situation on the Russian front was desperate, and the Tigers were pitched straight into action. Massive tank duels, the bitter one-to-one combats, and tank battles against anti-tank guns were the daily work of Michael Wittmann. His first great moment of triumph came in the titanic battle of Kursk.

THE ELEFANT

The Tiger may have proved itself to be a good design, but the first tank destroyer which was based on it was a misguided failure; this was the 'Elefant'.

The gun was mounted on the Tiger (P) chassis, a discarded prototype version of the Tiger made by Porsche. It incorporated twin gasoline generating units with direct electric drive. Although protected by heavy armour, this vehicle was unsuccessful, not least because it was ponderous and difficult to manoeuvre.

Like the Panther, this vehicle was rushed through the production stage so that it could be ready for the Kursk offensive. One major design flaw was the lack of a machine gun to back up the main gun, which was to have serious consequences for crews during battle. The suspension was also under immense strain due to the weight of the vehicle and resulted in the vehicle getting easily hogged down.

THE ATTACK ORDERS

Positioned on the opposite side of the turret from the gunner was the loader. He did the heavy manual work of loading the gun.

Although the orders for the preparation of the assault were issued in April, the actual attack did not take place until three months later in July. The delays were for a number of reasons. Hitler wanted no room for failure, so the plans were revised again and again to ensure no detail had been left out. In addition, the Führer had an almost child-like faith in the power of new weapons. He believed that the new generation of Panzers would win the war and he wanted the new Panthers and Elefants to be used in the battle. Despite the fact that the field trials of these new Panzers were not complete, they were committed to the battle anyway. This decision would prove costly during the ensuing clashes. The delays caused further, unforeseen problems. The Russians had been made aware of the German plans through the help of the 'Lucy' spy ring that had been passing decoded Ultra messages from Bletchley Park in England. They could also observe the massive German preparations for the battle and they began to make plans.

Initially Stalin had ordered a Soviet offensive to be launched to thwart the German plans. His generals, however, had persuaded him to adopt a defensive stance instead. The idea was to draw the German armoured forces into a well-prepared trap and destroy them with anti-tank defences. When they were on the point of destruction, a heavy armoured counter-attack would be launched to finish them off. The Russians knew that the Germans would be concentrating large amounts of armour in the area, so particular attention was paid to anti-tank defences. Anti-tank guns and anti-tank mines were laid out in pre-prepared areas that would blunt the German armour as they tried to punch through. The Russian defences overall consisted of extensive lines of trenches, minefields and pre-prepared killing grounds. These were arranged one behind the other and presented a formidable obstacle. The number of mines laid was as high as 5,000 per mile in some areas.

ANTI-TANK MEASURES

By 1943 a tank was no place to be. Infantry had, by now, developed extra killing power in the form of magnetic mines, Bazookas and the Panzerfausts. These deadly weapons could all blast through the armour of a tank. Early in the war the Russians found that the simple expedient of a bottle filled with petrol, lighted and thrown onto the engine decks, could disable even the largest tanks. Their tank-hunting teams soon became very adept at wielding this simple improvised device.

The ever-present danger for tanks was less spectacular than the anti-tank guns and tank-hunting teams, but equally deadly. Anti-tank mines could be placed in great numbers to protect a defensive position. These mines would support the weight of a man without detonating, so infantry teams often passed by unsuspecting, but as soon as the weight of a tank was sensed it would explode with tremendous force.

Although tanks were sometimes destroyed by mines, the most frequent result was that they lost a track. This resulted in crews having to leave their vehicle to attempt to repair these massive iron tracks in the heat of battle.

The job of testing for mines and clearing a path through them was the job of the Pioneer sections. Occasionally, this vital task was given insufficient time and care. At Kursk, General Heinz Guderian, the inspector of armour in the German Army at the time of the crucial battle, was left livid with rage. His new Tiger tanks had rolled into action through uncleared minefields, with the result that many of his most effective machines, the spearhead of the Army, were rendered immobile by a threat which could easily have been anticipated and cleared.

THE PRELUDE TO KURSK

During the three-month delay before the battle, the Russians had pushed vast amounts of men and material into the area. They also enlisted the help of an 'Army' consisting of hundreds of thousands of civilian helpers from the surrounding areas to construct the defensive trenches needed. When completed, these trenches would stretch for over six thousand miles. A vast number of civilians also helped construct a new rail line that would be used when the counter-attack was launched.

Over 20,000 artillery pieces were moved into the area by the Soviets, together with over 3,000 tanks, 2,000 planes and over one million men. The Russians had General Vatutin's Voronezh Front and General Rokossovsky's Central Front in the salient. In reserve would be General Konev's Steppe Front. The brilliant tactician Marshall Zhukov was in overall command. One mistake that the Russians made was in the assessment of where the main German attack would fall. They believed that it would come from the north and they arranged

Tiger tanks roll along a muddy road in the southern sector of the front during the first rains of autumn 1943. By now the Tiger had become established as a symbol of German tank power on the Eastern Front. Although only 1700 of these machines were ever manufactured, they were to forge a legend out of all proportion to their relatively samll numbers.

their forces accordingly. This resulted in a very tough defensive wall that would meet Model's forces head on. However, the Germans had assembled their main attacking forces in the south as part of Hoth's 4th Panzer Army. This would cause the Russians some real headaches in the days ahead.

The opening stages of the battle began just before 5am on the morning of the 5th July 1943. Through their highly developed intelligence sources, the Russians knew when the Germans were going to launch their attack. In a well-planned move, Zhukov ordered the Soviets to launch a pre-emptive artillery barrage. This strike had the desired result of catching the Germans out in the open during the forming stage. The ensuing panic and destruction offered a taste of what was to come. To add to the carnage, the Germans now launched their artillery strike. The resulting noise and destruction presented a devastating and awe-inspiring sight. Although lasting less than one hour in total, this opening phase reached new heights of ferocity. The Russian artillery bombardment delayed the start of the German attack, which did get under way about two hours late, with the infantry leading the way.

With the 9th Army in the north, Field Marshall Model had four Panzer Divisions to call on, the 2nd, 9th, 18th and 20th Panzer Divisions, plus three Heavy Tank Battalions. The heavy tank battalions consisted of the 505th

Heavy Tank Battalion equipped with 30 Tigers and the 653rd and 654th Heavy Tank Battalions equipped with a total of 90 of the new Ferdinand heavy tank destroyer. The emphasis of the German attack lay in the south with General Hoth's 4th Panzer Army and Army Detachment Kempf. There were a total of nine infantry Divisions in this area, together with the Grossdeutchland Panzer Grenadier Division and the SS Panzer Divisions Leibstandarte Adolf Hitler, Das Reich and Totenkopf. The four SS Divisions each had an attached Kompanie of 15 Tigers. The Leibstandarte and Das Reich Divisions were also equipped with the new Panthers. The crack Grossdeutchland Division was also equipped with a Tiger Kompanie and a number of Panthers. To back this already powerful armoured force up, the 503rd Heavy Tank Battalion was also allocated to this section with a further 45 Tigers. This made for a very impressive line-up and represented the best that Germany had to offer at that time, both in men and machines. One important feature that the Germans lacked was a suitable reserve force. The Russians had a very sizeable reserve to call upon, but the Germans had been badly mauled by two years of fighting in Russia.

It was not just on the ground that new German weapons were being tested. One important new development made its arrival from the air during the Kursk offensive. Hans-Ulrich Rudel, the famous Stuka pilot, was responsible for battle-testing a new addition to the Stuka that would prove itself a menace for the Red Army tank men. A pair of 37mm Flak cannon were fitted to the underside of the aircraft. It was found that this weapon was very accurate and very effective at destroying enemy tanks from the air. To make this new weapon work, however, the pilot had to go into a shallow dive and get within close range of his target, a task that presented its own dangers, but it worked, and the number of Russian tanks that fell to this new weapon grew steadily throughout the Kursk offensive.

THE OFFENSIVE BEGINS

As the offensive began to gather momentum, the 9th Army began their advance along the main Orel to Kursk railway line. They quickly ran into the first defensive line and the number of casualties began to rise. Within the first two days the 9th Army's attack was halted near Olkhovatka. They had advanced only 12 miles from their start point, but the concentration of the Russian forces in this sector had proved fatal for Model's forces. The revitalised Russian air force also helped to defeat the advance.

To compound the problems, in the North the new German tanks that had been expected to yield excellent results had performed miserably in battle. The Elefants started well, and had advanced only a few miles into enemy territory. Initially, the thick frontal armour proved a good defence against enemy attempts to disable them but, lacking a machine gun, they could not completely neutralise enemy infantry positions without supporting efforts. Accurate, sustained fire from the Soviet positions prevented the German infantry from following behind the tanks. The Ferdinands ran into difficulties when they became separated from their infantry support. The disastrous failure to fit an on-board machine gun prevented them from defending themselves against the enemy infantry. The Russians were able to get up close and disable or capture these new machines.

A different series of problems were visited on the Panther-equipped companies. Many of these tanks broke down on their way to the start point. Another worrying problem for the Panther crews was the fact that many of them actually caught fire, due to a badly designed exhaust system that accumulated unburned fuel. This first model of the Panther earned the nickname of 'Guderian's problem child'. Around 200 of these new tanks were sent to the Kursk area, and most broke down. The Tigers too experienced problems, especially with the retrieval of vehicles which were damaged by the extensive Russian minefields, which had been insufficiently cleared.

TANK RECOVERY

With the huge weight of the later war tanks, such as the Tiger, immobilised tanks could often only be moved by the power of another Tiger. The heaviest tractor in the German Army was the 18-ton Famo, but it took three of these harnessed together to move one broken down Tiger, and in the midst of the battlefield the tractors were highly vulnerable to anti-tank rounds, high explosive shells and the hand held weapons of the infantry.

The Tiger tanks, which each weighed about 60 tons, were prone to a range of mechanical and electrical failures. In addition, they were extremely expensive

An artist's impression from Signal magazine pays tribute to the services of the mobile workshops, which kept the Panzers in the field. Without these back-up services tank formations soon ground to a halt.

valuable assets that could not afford to be wasted. Because of this, recovering Tiger tanks was particularly important. There were a range of options available to the SS and the Army Tank Battalions which operated Tigers. Most obviously, they could use their own gun tanks to tow other tanks out of trouble. The problem with this is that it tended to cause electrical, engine or transmission malfunctions in the Tigers doing the towing. Alternatively, un-armoured half-tracks could be used, but unfortunately several of these needed to be used to tow a single Tiger, and because they were un-armoured they were vulnerable. Quite clearly what one required was an armoured recovery vehicle that could tow a Tiger on its own and which was capable of operating in intense combat conditions.

Once again, the solution to the problem was to develop a specialist recovery vehicle, known as a Bergenpanzer. These machines dispensed with the turret and replaced it with a box-like wooden structure. They were designed to run quickly up to disabled tanks and tow them away from enemy reach. Every tank carried heavy towing cables ready to be hitched up to a recovery vehicle or a friendly tank. Most sensible commanders went into action with their cables already hooked up, just in case.

The Tiger tanks may have looked incredibly robust, but in many respects they were surprisingly vulnerable. They required high maintenance, and also shed their caterpillar tracks with infuriating regularity, especially in thick mud, when crossing obstacles, or as a result of anti-tank fire and minefields. Veteran Jerry Majeuski recalled the problems with the Tigers:

"Tank tracks, as you might guess, are the most important part on a tank and they frequently had to be changed. For instance, if one link just breaks one pin, you haven't got a track any more. From enemy action tracks are often hit by enemy shells and damaged and have to be changed. It is a very hard job and takes a lot of effort to do it. The whole crew is involved. I've never done it myself under enemy action but I shudder to think what it would take."

In the south, Hoth's forces got off to a better start than Model's. The Tigers were placed at the head of the advance with the Panthers providing flank cover; the weaker Panzer IIIs and IVs came in behind in what was known as a 'Panzer-Kiel', or armoured-wedge. The Russians had spread out their forces in the south. This helped the 4th Panzer Army to make relatively good progress. By the end of day one, the 4th Panzer Army had advanced 15 miles to the town of Prokhorovka. The advance slowed considerably after this as the Russians poured in waves of reserves to meet the threat. As the advance slowed, the emphasis of the attack was shifted northwards. The SS Divisions had reached, and forced a crossing of, the Psel River by 11th July, bringing them close to the town of Prokhorovka. They prepared to advance further as Army Detachment Kempf moved parallel to their left flank, about 12 miles from their positions.

On the day that the great battle began, Wittmann destroyed eight tanks, and in the following tank battles he emerged as an unmatched tank ace. He overran batteries, picked out even the most cleverly camouflaged anti-tank gun nests, and constantly out-fought enemy tanks. He was cautious when he had to be, aggressive when it paid off, his keen hunter instincts, combined with a huge slice of luck, allowed him to emerge unscathed through five furious days of the biggest tank battles in history. Over and over again enemy tanks went up like blazing torches before him, and when Michael Wittmann washed his sweaty, powder-smeared face on the evening of the fifth day of battle, he knew that he had left behind him 30 wrecked T-34s, and had destroyed 28 Soviet anti-tank guns and two batteries of artillery.

By the 11th July Hoth's forces were only 12 miles from the town of Oboyan. This was where the Russians had centred their defences for the whole of the southern part of the Kursk salient, and the Germans knew that this area was a Russian strongpoint. Army Detachment Kempf was fighting to the southeast, towards Rzhavets. Hoth planned to turn to the east, away from Oboyan, and destroy the enemy to the south. He could then link with Kempf's forces and force a new path towards Kursk. The town that lay in Hoth's way was Prokhorovka. Success at Prokhorovka was essential to the continuation of the German advance.

Up to 12th July 1943, Prokhorovka was an unknown village. By the end of that day it would earn its place in the history of the Second World War. The Russians, who could see the threat posed by the SS-led armoured advance, poured strong armoured reserves into this area. Among these reserves was the 5th Guards Tank Army who were placed northeast of Prokhorovka alongside 5th Guards Army. The 5th Guards Tank Army could boast a strength of 850 various tanks including T34s and KV-ls. At this stage the Russians estimated that the German armoured advance consisted of 700 vehicles. The truth, however, was very different. Hoth's SS force had been severely weakened by the advance through the extensive enemy defences. By 11th July the II SS Panzer Korps could only muster 300 battle ready machines and a further 230 German armoured vehicles were fighting to their left with the rest of Hoth's forces. One major failure on the part of the Germans was that they failed to detect the formidable enemy force that lay in wait for them. Hoth felt confident that the enemy had been severely weakened and that the German attack would open up the east flank and push the enemy back towards Oboyan. All of this assembled armour was situated in an area of less than three square miles.

The start of the great armoured clash was preceded by air attacks launched by both sides. The Russians also delivered an artillery attack towards the German lines. This was quickly followed by the start of the Russian tank advance. Almost at the same time the Germans moved from their start points towards the Russian lines. The two sides met head on and a state of extreme confusion soon developed. Any hope of control over these formations was lost as both sides locked horns in a struggle for survival. At such short range the German Tigers and Panthers could not rely upon their far superior, long-range guns. The T-34s and other Russian machines found that they could destroy the German monsters as easily as they could be destroyed themselves. Also, in acts of suicide, Russian tanks were seen driving straight into the Tigers and ramming them, the resultant explosion assuring the complete destruction of both machines. In addition the planes and artillery from both sides could not play any part in deciding the outcome, as the danger of destroying friendly forces was too great.

The entire battle had lasted for 12 hours. In this short space of time the finest Divisions in Hitler's Army had been fought to a standstill. They had suffered heavy infantry casualties and could not break through the Russian lines. At the end of this time both sides settled back and assumed defensive positions. They both counted their losses and decided what to do next. The battle at Prokhorovka had resulted in losses for the Germans, but contrary to popular belief, these losses amounted to no more than 150 machines in total. The Germans managed to keep their battle-ready tank numbers at a fairly even number around this period; the majority of their losses had taken place in the first few days of the Kursk offensive. After Prokhorovka, the Germans simply lacked the strength and forces necessary to continue the advance. By this stage they were completely exhausted. The Russian tank losses during

The Pz.Kpfw VI - The Tiger was the long awaited solution to the qualitative advantages enjoyed by Soviet armour in the Russian campaign. There were never enough manufactured to overcome the massive advantages in numbers that the Soviet forces enjoyed.

Prokhorovka stood at around 400 tanks and this spelt a temporary setback in this area for them. In the overall plan they knew that they had yet to deliver the main attack elsewhere. Throughout the night of 12th July, the Russians and Germans recovered what vehicles they could from Prokhorovka and returned them to the repair shops in an attempt to make their losses good. The engineers destroyed whatever could not be recovered. Smaller scale fighting did continue in this area for the next few days, but the fact was that both the Russians and Germans were exhausted. Hitler called off the Zitadelle offensive on 13th July.

For a number of reasons 12th July 1943 proved a decisive day. Two days earlier on 10th July the Allies invaded the island of Sicily. This had been achieved with complete surprise and the invading force consisted of over 3,000 ships, a force that the thinly stretched resources of Germany could never hope to match. By the 12th the Allies had landed over 150,000 men and over 500 tanks on the island. Germany did not have the forces available to defeat this new threat. Hitler was now faced with the one thing he had tried desperately to avoid: a two-front war. There was worse to come.

As the clash of tanks was taking place at Prokhorovka, the Russians were preparing for the counter-attack in other areas. They had amassed a formidable attacking force in the north of the salient. Even as the German offensive continued, they began their probing attacks on 12th July, near Orel. The Germans began to fall back under the weight of this attack. They were weakened beyond repair and on top of this Hitler withdrew the elite 1st SS Panzer Division and sent them south towards the new threat in Italy. At the start of August, the Russian offensive began in full. It quickly gained ground and less than a week after the start of the attack, the Russians had retaken most of the lost areas. By the end of August they even managed Kharkov. This was the fourth and last time this Russian city would change hands. In some areas the going was tough for the Russians. The Germans had dug in well and got the chance to exact a measure of revenge for the losses they had endured. Von Manstein himself directed these defensive battles but the end was now in sight.

Germany had thrown the very best of its armoured forces into this battle in an attempt to win the decisive victory it needed. Hitler had placed all of his hopes in the Waffen-SS formations that had won him victory at Kharkov in March. He ensured that they were given preference in receiving the new Panthers and Tigers, but not even these new heavy tanks could win the day. At the end of this struggle these units, together with the rest of the forces involved, had suffered heavy losses in men and machines. This was to be the last offensive operation mounted by the Germans in the east. What it spelt for the Germans was the start of the end of the Russian campaign. The Armies of Adolf Hitler faced a one-way move back towards their homeland. Local successes did take place, but they were not enough to alter the final outcome.

For the Russians, it allowed them to seize the decisive advantage over the Germans. The carefully planned counter-attack tore large gaps in the German front line. They had at last proved that the mighty German Army was beatable. With regards to tanks, sheer numerical superiority overwhelmed the technical superiority of the Panthers and Tigers. This victory did provide a beacon for the whole world; the victory however, lay not with the forces of Hitler, but with the forces of Stalin.

Despite these reverses, Michael Wittmann continued his success in late autumn. Near Brusilov he ran into a Soviet tank assembly area, taking the enemy by surprise, and in that single action, blasted ten tanks from the mass of Soviet armour. Three more fell prey to his Tiger later that afternoon. Wittmann marked every tank eliminated, but he rated the anti-tank guns he destroyed twice as high. He hated these concealed nests, which he called 'the hiding places of death'. By this stage of the war, Wittmann professed that enemy tanks had ceased to be a strain on his nerves, and only the anti-tank guns still made him uncomfortable.

The Nazi propaganda department were naturally keen to capitalise on Wittmann's success and a war writer was sent to join him in his tank. He filed this report:

'In an attack against a large town guarded strongly by tanks and anti-tank guns, we cleared the way rather quickly by destroying several tanks and anti-tank guns and soon reached the town. Our targets were all to the right of our direction of travel, from our twelve to approximately three o'clock positions. Suddenly to our left, behind a haystack, we sighted a Joseph Stalin I with its gun trained on us. Wittmann: "Turn left, target 100 metres, go!". And that was it'.

This action resulted in the destruction of 15 enemy tanks in a single day. Wittmann frequently manoeuvred the Tiger based on his experience in assault guns. From a static position, he would swing the whole vehicle round, rather than waste time moving the turret. Moving the Tiger in this way was accomplished by one track turning forward and the other in reverse. This called for extreme caution with the Tiger however, because of the great danger of shedding one of the huge tracks while turning in place, which could cause soil to accumulate under the idler wheels and the tracks to snap.

Unlike most tank crews, Wittmann's gunner, 'Bobby' Woll, often fired without a target designation from his commander, for, as Wittmann frequently put it, there was no time for a conversation, and Bobby Woll often acquired the target in the few split seconds which meant the difference between life and death.

On 15th January 1944 armoured groups of Leibstandarte and Das Reich Divisions were ordered to drive further northwest in the direction of Ljubar. This armoured advance was stopped, principally by heavy fire from anti-tank guns and mortars. These two days of intense fighting saw Wittmann destroy six enemy tanks, 20 anti-tank guns, 60 guns, 32 trucks and countless other vehicles. On 16th January 1944 both Wittmann and Bobby Woll received the Knight's Cross. Woll was the first soldier holding rank as low as gunner to be awarded such a high decoration. There were now two wearers of the Knight's Cross in Wittmann's Tiger.

As a member of Wittmann's crew, Woll's success surpassed that of every other gunner in the winter battles of 1943 and 1944.

By January, he had destroyed 80 tanks and 107 anti-tank guns. Bobby Woll played an important part in the success of Michael Wittmann. With his quick reactions and good eye, he was a master behind the mighty '88' gun. Confident of Woll's ability, Wittmann was not intimidated and would often take on superior numbers of enemy tanks. The two made a fine team and Woll knew Wittmann's ways to the letter. While a crew's driver, radio operator and loader often changed, the commander and gunner stayed together whenever possible.

Making up the rest of Wittmann's crew in January 1944 were Werner Irrgang (radio operator), Eugen Schmidt (driver) and Sepp Robner (loader).

Balthasar Woll, Michael Wittmann's Tiger gunner, used a rather idiosyncratic method; he preset his sights to 800m, which was the kind of average length or distance at which a Tiger would engage a target. He would then correct the targets that were closer or further away using his great experience and essentially intuition in order to fire the gun either higher or lower than the point which was directed by the sight, a very quick and efficient way of firing the gun.

The Tigers were feared by the Soviets and the heavy German tanks often drew heavy anti-tank fire in their attacks. They were used as weapons to smash gaps in enemy positions for the grenadiers to move up in support. In countless attacks they breached anti-tank fronts and destroyed enemy artillery positions. With their high rate of fire, they could out-fight any tank on the battlefield. Although few in number, the Tigers performed outstanding feats in the offensive and defensive roles. Constantly under a hail of fire from anti-tank rifles, anti-tank guns and rocket launchers, the Tigers did not get off unscathed. However, thanks to their strong frontal armour they were difficult to knock out. Often shells fired by enemy tanks and anti-tank guns simply bounced off. Nevertheless, the Tiger was not invulnerable, and losses always kept pace with the slow trickle of new machines arriving at the front from the hard-pressed German factories.

The incredible achievements of Wittmann on the battlefield did not go unnoticed. He was fast becoming a national hero. On 2nd February 1944 he was summoned to Hitler's headquarters. Michael Wittmann received the Knight's Cross with Oak Leaves from the hand of Adolf Hitler. In the course of his conversation with Wittmann, Hitler noticed that he was missing a front tooth. He subsequently sent him to his dentist to have the tooth replaced.

CAPTURED SOVIET TANKS T-34/76

When captured - as a large number were - the T-34/76 was designated by the Germans as Panzerkampfwagen T-34 747(r). The Germans were always more than happy to employ as many captured examples as they could and many served with various units. The first examples of captured T-34/76 were in service with 1st, 8th and 11th Panzer Divisions during the summer of 1941,

Captured Russian T-34 tanks were sent into action with German markings. This cuold prove a hazardous introduction as frequently German anti-tank teams opened fire at the first sighting of this familiar silhouette without looking to identify the markings.

although the crews considered it a dangerous undertaking to utilise captured T-34/76 tanks as many anti-tank gunners fired on sight of the feared T-34 silhouette rather than waiting to see the exact markings. In order to prevent such mistakes the crews of captured T-34s painted large crosses and swastikas on the turret. It was also very common to paint a cross or swastika on top of the turret in order to prevent the Luftwaffe from attacking. Another way to overcome this problem was to use captured T-34/76s in an infantry support role, where recognition problems were less common. The T-34/76D (model 1943) tanks with round twin turret hatches were often nicknamed 'Mickey Mouse' by the Germans because of their comic appearance when both hatches were open.

From late 1941 onwards, captured T-34/76 tanks were transported to a workshop in Riga for repairs and modifications, while in 1943 Mercedes-Benz in Marienfelde and Wumag in Goerlitz (now Zgorzelec) were also repairing and modifying T-34s. Captured T34/76 tanks were modified to German standards by the installation of a commander's cupola and radio equipment. Other non-standard field modifications were also made by the their new crews. Spare parts were never a significant problem and some 300 captured vehicles were maintained on a long-term basis. T-34/76s tanks were also used as artillery tractors and ammunition carriers, and badly damaged tanks were either dug in as pillboxes or used for testing and training purposes.

Known users of captured T-34/76 tanks were numerous, although there were probably countless occasions on which these machines were used but not recorded. As early as 15th October 1941 the 1st Panzer Division had six T-34/76 tanks. T-34/76 tanks were also in service with the 2nd Panzer Division, 9th Panzer Division, 10th Panzer Division, 20th Panzer Division and the 23rd Panzer Division. A number of T-34/76 tanks were still in service in 1945, for example with the 23rd Panzer Division in Slovakia and East Prussia. In the summer of 1943, a few captured T-34/76 tanks were even operated by Italian crews. According to original German captured tank inventories, as of July 1943 there were 28 T-34(r) serving as part of Army Group South and 22 as part of Army Group Centre. In September of 1943, a RONA (Russian Army of Liberation) unit commanded by Mieczyslaw Kaminski operated some 24 captured T-34/76 tanks against Soviet partisans in Byelorussia. Even elite units such as Panzergrenadier Division 'Grossdeutschland' used some captured examples as late as 1945. The Waffen SS units too did not hesitate to use captured T-34/76 tanks and both the 2nd SS Panzer Division 'Das Reich' and the 3rd SS Panzer Division 'Totenkopf ' are known to have pressed significant numbers into service. T-34/76 tanks used by 'Das Reich' are of particular interest. When in March 1943, the lst SS Panzer Corps recaptured Kharkov, 50 models of the T-34/76 tank were captured. All of these had been undergoing repair in a local tractor factory that was overrun and re-designated as the SS Panzerwerk (SS Tank Workshop). Shortly afterwards they were repaired and modified to German standards, repainted and given German markings. Modifications included the installation of commander's cupola (from damaged Panzerkampfwagen III and IV tanks), and the addition of Schurzen (armour skins). Other equipment such as Notek light, storage boxes, tools, radio equipment and new radio antenna was also added. Twenty-five of these machines entered service with the newly created 3rd SS Panzer Baltalion of the 2nd SS Panzer Regiment 'Das Reich'. SS Hauptscharführer Emil Seibold from the 3rd SS Panzer Battalion scored 69 kills during his career, including a number using his Panzerkampfwagen T-34 747(r) in July and August of 1943, during the Battle of Kursk Salient. Seibold received the Knight's Cross during the last decoration ceremony on 6th May 1945. The 3rd SS Panzer Division 'Totenkopf' also pressed a number of captured T-34s into service and there were at least twenty-two T-34/76 tanks in service with this SS Panzer Division during the Battle of Kursk Salient, which means that 'Totenkopf' probably fielded more T-34s than Tigers!

On 30th December 1944, some 29 Panzerkampfwagen T-34 747(r) were in service with 100th Gebirgsjager Regiment. In 1942, a single T-34/76 and KV-2 were used to form 661 Panzer Company for the planned invasion of Malta. Two T-34/76 tanks were certainly captured by Schwere Panzer Abteilung 502 on the Leningrad Front in November 1943 and were pressed into service. There were also some T-34/76 tanks in service with Hermann Göring Fallschirm-Panzer Division which took part in the suppression of the Warsaw Uprising in 1944. In the summer of 1944 the Germans sold three captured T-34/76 tanks to Finland.

LATE WAR CAPTURED TANKS

Late in 1943 an improved model of the T-34 operated by a five-man crew and armed with an 85mm gun and machine gun was introduced. It was designated as T-34/85 and by the end of the war 29,430 of these tanks were produced. Only a few were captured and even fewer actually made it into German service. On 6th September 1944, the 5th SS Panzer Division 'Viking', during heavy fighting on the Vistula front near Warsaw (north of Serock), captured two T-34/85 tanks and used them in action. The 252nd Infantry Division, during their combat in East Prussia, also used a captured T-34/85 in battle.

SELF-PROPELLED ARTILLERY

Once again the US Handbook on the German Army of 1945 provides a good insight into how German armour was viewed by the Allies. The correct use of self-propelled artillery from 1943 onwards excited considerable interest from the Allies, and this contemporary record clearly illustrates the Allied concern over these machines, which first began to make a real impact around the time of the battle of Kursk:

DEVELOPMENT

"German self-propelled artillery has now developed to a point where there is scarcely any artillery piece up to and including 150mm calibre which has not appeared on at least one self-propelled chassis. Some of these have been experimental, but others have been standardised and have appeared in large numbers.

PRODUCTION METHODS

"Self-propelled artillery has been produced in three different ways. First, there are the gun-chassis combinations which have been designed and engineered carefully to fill a particular role. These were produced in quantity by major armament factories in Germany and exist in large numbers. The 75mm and 105mm assault guns are examples of this type. Second, there are the standard guns fitted on standard tank chassis. Conversion has been carried out in accordance with well-engineered designs at considerable expense of time and skill. Among these are the 10.5cm le. F. H. 1812 on the Gw. II (Wespe) and the 15cm s. F. 11. 1811 on the Gw. III/IV (Hummel). Third, there is a large class of self-propelled guns produced by field conversion, carried out in unit or base workshops, and requiring little skill, time or material. An example of this is the 15cm s. I. G. 33 mounted on the chassis of the Pz. Kpfw. I

TACTICAL USES

"German self-propelled artillery may be divided into four types from a tactical point of view, but the line of demarcation often is not clear, as many self propelled artillery pieces have dual missions. These types are: close-support artillery, including assault guns; field and medium artillery; tank destroyers; and anti-aircraft artillery.

"Close-support and assault guns. The development of close-support and assault guns was begun about 1940. Assault guns are designed for the close support of infantry, and normally consist of a gun of limited traverse on an armoured self-propelled chassis carrying heavy frontal armour. They are inclined to be slower and less manoeuvrable than tanks but are suited particularly well for attacks on enemy infantry heavy weapons and main points of resistance.

"Field and medium self-propelled artillery. Field and medium self-propelled artillery was introduced first about the middle of 1942. Both types of howitzers (10.5cm. le F. H. 18 and 15cms. F. H. 18) in the Division artillery now may be found on self-propelled chassis.

"Self-propelled anti-tank guns. The first self-propelled anti-tank gun was the 4.7cm PAK. (t) mounted on the then (1941) obsolescent chassis of the Pz. Kpfw I b.) Anti-tank guns now form the numerically largest class of self-propelled artillery weapons.

"Self-propelled anti-aircraft artillery. Self-propelled anti-aircraft artillery initially was developed before any attempt was made to apply this principle to other types of weapons, but so far no serious effort has been made to mount anti-aircraft guns larger than 37mm on motor-driven carriages.

GUN AND CHASSIS MODIFICATIONS

"Guns, with the exception of assault guns, are mounted normally on their self-propelled carriages without any major alteration. Assault guns usually are fitted with electric firing devices and modified recoil systems. The chassis, however, particularly in cases where they are those of existing tanks, have undergone considerable modification. Not only have the superstructures been altered, but in some cases the engine has been moved from the rear to a central position to enable the gun crew to stand on the floor of the hull to serve the gun."

ALLIED TANK LOSSES

It has been estimated that from May 1944 until the end of the war, on any given day, on average, only 600 tanks were available for action in the entire German Army. The Allies could call on some 20,000.

With this tremendous disparity in numbers, the German Tank Divisions would had to have destroyed ten Russian tanks for every one of their own lost.

Two Panzer IVs and a Marder tank-destroyer are shown in action during the intense battles which led to the recapture of Kharkov.

In fact, by the end of the war it is estimated that five Russian tanks were destroyed for every German tank. But it was never enough to affect the huge numerical superiority enjoyed by the Allies. Even on the Western Front, four Allied tanks were being destroyed for every German machine lost.

For the Western Allies, the solution was very much the same as the Russians. It was to abandon the search for tactical advances, take a simple workable design and manufacture it in vast quantities. The Allied option was the Sherman. It had numerous flaws, chief among them its very high profile, which made an easy target, but it was available in huge numbers. So many Shermans were manufactured that they were even shipped to the East to help the Russian war effort. The Russian response was politely muted as the Sherman never matched the standards of the T-34. Even when it was upgraded to include a high velocity 85mm weapon, the tank was really no match for the new breed of German armour such as the Tiger. As further proof of the Sherman's weakness, it is interesting to note that only a small proportion of Tiger tanks were actually destroyed by Allied tanks. The vast majority either fell victim to Allied fighter-bombers or had to be abandoned and destroyed by their crews when they experienced mechanical difficulties, or, more frequently, ran out of fuel.

From 1944 the Allied bombing campaigns were really beginning to bite and the shortage of fuel and spare parts was killing the Panzer formations as effectively as the Allied Armies were.

PANZERKAMPFWAGEN V
SD.KFZ.171

By the end of the first year of the war it was clear that the Panzer IIs and IIIs were not suitable for combat with stronger British, French and Russian tanks. In 1941, Hitler decided that a prototype for a 'heavy' tank should be designed to provide the German Army with heavier fighting vehicles. The result was the Panzer V Panther and possibly the most well-known and outstanding German tank of World War II.

From the two prototypes designed by MAN and Daimler-Benz, the MAN design was the one which went into production. Initially, Hitler preferred the Daimler-Benz design but it was rejected by the "Panther Committee" on account of identification problems with the vehicle. By the end of 1942 a pre-production series of 20 tanks were produced under the name Null-Serie. They were designated as PzKpfw V Panther Ausf A; lightly armoured (60mm frontal armour), deployed a 75mm KwK 42 L/70 gun and were powered by

Panther Ausf. D tanks photographed in 1943.

The Panther endured an inauspicious birth at Kursk but it was to become one of the best medium tanks of the war.

a Maybach HL2 10 P45 engine. Technically, these early versions were very different from later prototypes in the series.

Also, by December 1942, a newly moderated version of the Panther, designated the Ausf D, was ready and had entered production. A month later the first Panzer Ausf D with improved armoured protection and re-versioned gun left the factory. The first 250 Panther Ausf Ds were also referred to as the Ausf D 1. These machines made their combat debut during Operation Citadel in July 1943, but due to technical problems many Panthers broke down in action and from the original 250 only 43 were in still service the following year.

Production of a further 600 Ausf D - designated Ausf D2 - had a more powerful HL230 P30 engine which then became standard for future models. In August 1943, the next model was the Ausf A instead of the expected Ausf E and between the four manufacturers of MAN, Daimler-Benz, MNH and DEMAG, 1,788 models were constructed.

Further modifications saw the next model, the Panther Ausf G, become the most numerous model with 3,740 being produced between March 1944 and April 1945 by MAN, Daimler-Benz and MNH. The hull was redesigned with thicker sides, the hatches for the hull gunner and driver were hinged making them easier to open, and the ammunition storage increased from 79 to 82 rounds.

A Panther on the Eastern Front in 1944.

In 1936, AEG were ordered to start the development of infrared night-vision devices, and in 1939 the first successful prototype unit was ready for use with 37mm Pak 35136 L/45 anti-tank gun. In autumn of 1942, a unit for use with 75mm PaK 40 L/46 anti-tank gun was constructed and was also mounted on Marder II (Sd.Kfz.l31).

In June 1943 tests started with infrared night-vision (Nacht Jager) devices and telescopic rangefinders mounted on a Panther. Two different arrangements were created and used on Panther tanks.

Solution A - Sperber (Sparrow Hawk) was made up of one 30cm infrared searchlight (with range of 600m) and image converter operated by the commander - FG 1250. From late 1944 to March of 1945, some Panzerkampfwagen V Panther Ausf G's (and other variants) mounted with FG 1250 were successfully tested. From March to April of 1945, approximately 50 Panther Ausf G's (and other variants) mounted with FG 1250 saw combat service on the Eastern and Western Fronts. Panthers with IR operated with SdKfz.251/20 Uhu (Owl) half-track with a 60cm infrared searchlight and Sd.Kfz.251/21 Falke (Falcon). This solution could easily be mounted on any type of armoured fighting vehicle.

Solution B - The second and more complicated arrangement was the "Biwa" (Bildwandler), which provided the driver, gunner and commander with one 30cm infrared searchlight (with a range of 600m) and image converter. Various variants of Panthers were converted and mounted with "Biwa". It was reported that tests were successful, but there were very few combat reports from the Eastern or Western Fronts.

In May 1944, the newly designed Ausf F was to be manufactured exclusively with steel-rimmed road-wheels and increased armour protection. The prototype Ausf G was completed in January 1945 and although it is possible that a few were completed and used in combat before the war ended, it is more commonly thought that only certain key components were ever assembled by Daimler-Benz.

CONVERSIONS

- **Befehlswagen Ausf D/A/G (Sd.Kfz.267)** - command tank
- **Befehlswagen Ausf D/A/G (Sd.Kfz.268)** - ground to air liason tank
- **Beobachtungspanzer Panther Ausf D** - observation tank
- **Bergepanther (Sd. Kfz. 179)** - recovery vehicle
- **Munisionspanzer Panther** - ammunition carrier
- **Panzerjager Jagdpather (Sd. Kfz. 173)**
- **Flakpanzer V Coelian** 2 x 37mm / 55mm Flak gun - planned
- **Flakpanzer V / Grille 10** - (lengthened chassis) - prototype
- **Grille 10** - 100mm K gun carrier (planned)
- **Grille 10** - 105mm leFH 43/35 (planned)
- **Minenraumpanzer Panther** - mine clearing tank (prototype stage)
- **Ramschaufelpanzer Panther** - dozer tank
- **Munition Schlepper Panther** (2 produced)
- **Munition Schlepper / Waffentrager Panther** - (shortened chassis - planned)
- **Grille 12** - 128mm K 43/44 gun carrier by Krupp (planned)
- **Skorpion** - 128mm K 43 gun carrier by Rhienmetal (planned)
- **Grille 15** - 150mm sFH 43/44 howitzer carrier (planned)
- **88mm Flakwagen Panther**

ARMOUR (mm/angle) Ausf G	
Front Turret: 110/11	Rear Turret: 45/25
Front Upper Hull: 80/55	Rear Lower Hull: 40/30
Front Lower Hull: 60/55	Turret Top/ Bottom: 16/84 16/90
Side Turret: 45/25	Upper Hull Top / Bottom: 40/90 16/90
Side Upper Hull: 50/30	Lower Hull Top / Bottom: 30/90 16/90
Side Lower Hull: 40/0	Gun Mantlet: 100/round

Model	Ausf D	Ausf A	Ausf G
Weight	44 tonnes	45.5 tonnes	44.8 tonnes
Crew	5	5	5
Engine	Maybach HL 230 P30 V-12 700 bhp	Maybach HL 230 P30 V-12 700 bhp	Maybach HL 230 P30 V-12 700 bhp
Speed	Road: 46 km/h	Road: 46 km/h	Road: 46 km/h
Range	Road: 160 km Crosscountry: 100 km	Road: 160 km Crosscountry: 100 km	Road: 160 km Crosscountry: 100 km
Fuel Capacity	730 litres	730 litres	730 litres
Length	6.87 m	6.87 m	6.87 m
Width	3.27 m	3.27 m	3.27 m
Height	2.95 m	3.1 m	2.95 m
Armament	L/70 & 2 x 7.92mm MG	L/70 & 3 x 7.92mm MG	L/70 & 3 x 7.92mm MG

The well sloped frontal armour of the Panther and the wide tracks were two features first seen in the T-34. At one stage it was suggested that the German army simply copied the T-34, but Hitler's pride overruled any further discussion.

Large numbers of self-propelled guns finally began to arrive at the front during 1943.

ACTION IN
ITALY AND NORMANDY

"In the West we suffered from a severe shortage of heavy weapons and particularly in tanks. Repeated crises in the East had constantly drawn away our tank strength. In June 1944 we were still using some French tanks which we had captured in 1940."

LIEUtTENANT-GENERAL BODO ZIMMERMAN, ON NORMANDY

On 25th July 1943 Benito Mussolini was arrested and Marshal Pietro Badoglio became his successor. On 8th September 1943 the Italian Government announced the armistice and Italy dropped out of its alliance with Germany. On 9th September 1943 the Germans quickly occupied Italy, the Italian armed forces were disarmed and equipment confiscated in Operation Achse (Axis). Following the operation Italy declared war on Germany on 13th September. On 15th September Mussolini's New Fascist State, the Salo Republic (or Italian Social Republic - Republica Sociale Italiana - RSI) was set up in Northern Italy and loyal forces continued fighting alongside the Germans until the end of the war. During Operation Axis, the Germans captured large number of Italian armoured fighting vehicles, the majority of which they were familiar with from North Africa. The Germans also occupied many of the Northern Italian plants where the Italian tanks were produced. In addition a large number of other vehicles was also captured. Some captured armoured fighting vehicles were handed over to the armed forces of the Italian Social Republic.

After the completely successful withdrawal from Sicily in 1943, the main focus of the German campaign in Italy lay in dogged defence and it was for this reason that armour was mainly deployed.

Outside of the powerful counter-attacks which were launched against the Allied landings at Salerno and Anzio the German tanks were chiefly used as mobile strong points. They were often dug into the ruins of buildings or carefully placed to cover one of the innumerable mountain passes which dotted the Italian countryside.

The US military handbook of 1945 provides a good insight into the German ability to put the lessons from the years of mobile war into the fight against superior numbers of Allied machines:

"ANTI-MECHANIZED DEFENCE"

"In constructing a defensive position the Germans stress construction of obstacles and anti-tank defences. If possible they select tank-proof terrain, and natural tank obstacles, such as steep slopes, are improved. Very steep forward slopes are made at least eight yards deep, while uphill slopes are made two to three yards high. Originally the Germans constructed anti-tank ditches well forward of the main line of resistance, but experience taught them that such ditches offered favourable jumping-off positions for hostile infantry and also revealed the location of the main line of resistance. At the present time, therefore, anti-tank ditches normally are dug in the area between the main line of resistance and the artillery positions. They are built in an uninterrupted line to avoid leaving passages that can be exploited by the enemy. All crossings essential to assure the manoeuvrability of friendly troops are built so that they can be blown up on the shortest notice.

"The Germans are aware that obstacles of any kind are effective only when covered by fire from various weapons. Consequently, there usually are trenches behind the anti-tank ditches from which machine gun and anti-tank-gun fire can cover the entire length of the tank obstacle.

"The Germans learned that dense minefields in front of their positions were an inadequate tank obstacle, because the enemy usually neutralised them by massed artillery fire or by concentrating air bombardment before launching a large-scale attack. Now German minefields normally are laid within the main battle position, and only single mines are dispersed in pattern at wide intervals in front of the main line of resistance. Particular stress is placed on the mining of roads. Routes of withdrawal which have to be left open are prepared for mining, and, if time does not permit placing of actual mines, dummy mines are installed.

"The Germans employ many kinds of tank obstacles. They recently have used static flamethrowers dug into the ground. Usually sited in pairs and in conjunction with other tank obstacles, they are fired by well-concealed personnel as soon as hostile tanks come within range.

"German anti-tank guns are disposed in depth, with some well forward. They often are dug in and carefully concealed to prevent the enemy from discovering the location and strength of the anti-tank defences prior to attack. In emplacing anti-tank guns, the Germans prefer positions in enfilade or on reverse slopes. They normally employ two to three anti-tank guns in each position, protecting them from infantry attacks with light machine guns. Ranges at which the Germans open fire upon hostile tanks vary according to the calibre of the gun and its position. Although single anti-tank guns sometimes engage enemy tanks at ranges up to 1,000 yards, main anti-tank defences usually hold their fire until the range is reduced to about 150 to 300 yards. The employment of close-combat anti-tank teams supplements the anti-tank defence. When the hostile tank attack is repulsed, the anti-tank guns move to alternate positions.

"The Germans emphasise that the use of smoke can be of great assistance in defeating enemy tank attacks. Smoke shells are fired into the attacking formation about one-third the distance back from the leading echelon. Thus the Germans avoid blinding their own anti-tank gunners, and leading hostile tanks not only are left without adequate support but are silhouetted against the smoke. The German also rely on the smoke being sucked into the tanks and forcing the crews to dismount."

THE DEFENCE OF ROME AGAINST THE GERMANS

The German forces fighting in Italy should have been augmented by Italian armour but, as we have seen, most of the Italian machines were of very little

Albert Speer and a group of technicians are seen here driving the chassis of the Tiger E Series. The Tiger proved itself to be well adapted to the strains of the Russian front; the wide tracks made it well-suited for driving through mud as Speer is in the process of demonstrating.

fighting value. The Carro Armato (Pesante) P26/40 four-man medium tank was the most modern tank in the Italian Army's arsenal, but only five pre-series vehicles were completed before German occupation. A single P26/40 was shown to Hitler on 20th October 1943 at Arys (in East Prussia) along with wooden mock-ups   of Panzerkampfwagen VI Tiger II Ausf. B (King Tiger) and Jagdpanzer VI Jagdtiger Ausf. B. None of the pre-series vehicles saw any combat with the Italian units and were issued to Panzer Ausbildung Abteilung South (training unit of Army Group C).

After the fall of Axis forces in North Africa on 13th May 1943 preparations for planned Operation Husky, the invasion of Sicily began. On 10th July 1943, the Allied landings took place and by 17th August 1943 Allied forces had reached Messina. Sicily provided the Allies with a first foothold in Europe, although the majority of German and Italian defenders were evacuated along with their equipment to the Italian mainland. On 3rd September 1943 the Allies crossed the Strait of Messina and invaded the Italian mainland. The Italian campaign, with its prolonged heavy fighting, did not have a significant impact on the course the course of the war other than the fact that it tied up a large number of German troops. The campaign ended on 2nd May 1945 when the last German units in Northern Italy surrendered.

During the Italian campaign Allied forces used a variety of armoured fighting vehicles, but it appears that only a small number were captured by the Germans. This can be explained by the fact that during the course of the campaign Germans were mainly on the defensive or were skilfully retreating.

THE WESTERN FRONT

The best indication of the Allied view of the qualities of German armour and armoured formations generally comes from the US Army handbook. As a document actually designed for those going into the field, we have an excellent view of the German forces through contemporary eyes.

It is interesting to note that the main lessons from the development of the German tank forces were already becoming apparent when this remarkably well-informed piece was being written in 1945:

"The story of German armoured vehicle development is concerned principally with tanks, which have undergone considerable change since the

A Panzer II advances deeper into Russia during the early phase of the campaign. By 1944 these tanks were obsolete but some were still in service in a policing role.

beginning of the war. German tanks have shown, in the course of five years of war, a gradual change from the Blitzkrieg concept of battle to greater emphasis on defensive, or at least offensive-defensive, operations for which the latest German tank, the King Tiger, heavily armed and armoured but relatively slow and unmanoeuvrable, was most suited.

"German tank development began in 1934, ostensibly at the same time as the rest of the rearmament program, but there is no doubt that considerable thought and experimentation had been devoted to the subject before them. By 1939 the Germans had evolved four types of tanks: the Pz. Kpfw. I, II, III and IV, with which the Blitzkrieg campaigns were conducted. There is evidence that larger tanks were being developed in 1939, and specimens of what are assumed to have been Pz. Kpfw. V. and a Pz. Kpfw. VI in an experimental stage were employed in the invasion of Norway. These, however, must have proved unsatisfactory, since they were dropped, and the present Pz. Kpfw. V (Panther) and Pz. Kpfw. VI (Tiger) have no connection with them.

"Meanwhile, the Pz. Kpfw. I and II gradually became obsolescent, first being relegated to reconnaissance roles and then finally disappearing in 1943 from the Table of Equipment of the Panzer regiment. The heavier tanks, Pz. Kpfw.

III and IV, which had proven satisfactory under fire, were modified to meet new conditions by thicker armour and more effective guns.

"In 1942, the Pz. Kpfw. VI. or Tiger, appeared in Russia, and later in Africa. The Tiger was designed in the direct German tradition, and simply was armed more heavily and armoured more thickly than its predecessors. It appeared out of its proper order in the line of succession, for the Pz. Kpfw. V. or Panther, did not appear until nearly a year later. The Panther was somewhat of a surprise, since it marked a departure from the conventional lines of German design, and in the arrangement of its armour showed strong signs of Russian influence. Its great success [Pz. Kpfw. is the German abbreviation for Panzerkampfwagen, meaning armoured fighting vehicle or tank] in combat undoubtedly gave rise to the decision to redesign the Tiger, which to some extent had fallen short of expectations. The new version is the Konigstiger or King Tiger."

OBSOLETE TANKS

"General, the Pz. Kpfw. I, Pz. Kpfw II, and Pz. Kpfw. III, although obsolete, are discussed here since they still may be met occasionally in the field.

LIGHT TANK (Pz. Kpfw. 1)

This was the first tank to be standardised by the Germans, and the first ones were produced in 1934. Three models (A, B, and C) and a commander's version (based on model B) have been identified, but model C never has been encountered in action. The hull of the Pz. Kpfw I was used as a self-propelled mount for several types of artillery weapons, but it no longer will be met even in this role.

LIGHT TANK (Pz. Kpfw. II)

This tank is manned by three men: a commander who acts as the gunner; a radio operator: and a driver. A large number of models of this tank were produced before it became obsolete. In a very much modified form it has reappeared as the Luchs (Lynx) reconnaissance tank in Western Europe. The original experimental models of Pz. Kpfw. II were produced between 1934 and 1936; it finally was abandoned as a fighting vehicle in 1943. A flame-throwing version, Pz. Kpfw. II (F), also has become obsolete and probably will not be met again. Model F, not the flame-thrower tank, was the latest model encountered. The modified hull of the Pz. Kpfw. II is still in use as a self-propelled gun carriage, notably in the case of the 15cm, S.I.G. 33 and the 10cm. Ie. F.H. 18.(2) Specifications.

MEDIUM TANK (Pz. Kpfw. III)

This tank has appeared in many models but has retained basic characteristics throughout. The latest models to appear are armed with the long-barrelled 5cm Kw.K. 39 (L/60), which in 1942 displaced the shorter 5cm Kw.K. (L/42). The original main armament, discarded late in 1940, was a 37-mm gun. The Pz. Kpfw. III now is obsolete and rarely encountered. The excellent hull and suspension have been utilised as the carriage for self-propelled guns, and it is in this form that the vehicle remains in production. The Pz. Kpfw. III has been encountered armed with the short 7.5 cm Kw.K. (the original armament of the Pz. Kpfw. IV), and also as a commander's vehicle, as a flame-throwing tank, as a wrecker tank, as an armoured ammunition carrier, and as an armoured observation post."

ANTI-AIRCRAFT TANKS

By 1944. the Allied air forces in the west enjoyed almost total air superiority. The Russia Air Force had recovered from its early defeats and was now almost as effective as the British and Americans. Vehicle losses reached catastrophic proportions as the fighter-bombers roared over the front looking for targets.

Now the real priority was for anti-aircraft protection, which could move with the tanks and give some cover against the relentless attacks of the Allied fighter-bombers. It was in this role that more Panzer IV conversions were made. These self-propelled anti-aircraft guns were produced in three forms. Firstly, there was the Möbelwagen (the troops nickname meant furniture van, because of its resemblance to a peacetime removal truck). Interestingly, the same nickname had earlier been used for the Tiger in response to its uncompromising flat-sided construction. The Möbelwagen was followed by two later machines, the Wirbelwind or Whirlwind, and Ostwind or East Wind.

In the case of the Möbelwagen, this was very much a wartime contingency measure, rather than a purpose-designed vehicle.

As damaged Panzer IVs were brought back for repair from the Eastern front, they were converted to an anti-aircraft role by the simple expedient of taking off the turret and replacing it with a 20mm flak gun which was protected, when in transit, by four collapsible sides, which were lowered when the flak gun was in action.

To say this was an unsuccessful design was an understatement, as the 20cm was no longer an effective anti-aircraft gun. Of even greater concern was the fact that the sides of the Möbelwagen had to be lowered to allow the gun to fire. This left the crew with no protection whatsoever, and defeated the whole purpose of mounting the gun on a tank chassis in the first place. The front line troops were quick to point out that, in action, the same result could have been achieved by placing an anti-aircraft gun on the back of a truck.

Miraculously, 240 conversions had been made before this glaring design flaw came to light. Effectively, 240 precious tanks had been wasted. A measure of effectiveness was achieved by increasing the size of gun from 20mm to 37mm, but the Möbelwagen was deemed a failure. It was obvious that what was required was an anti-aircraft vehicle that gave the crew the benefits of armour protection while they were in action.

The immediate solution was the Wirbelwind. It used the Panzer IV chassis and four 20mm flak guns in a quad arrangement, now mounted on a fully rotating turret which gave the crew some measure of protection.

Even mounted in groups of four, the 20mm flak gun was still ineffectual against the heavily armoured Allied aircraft, so the Wirbelwind was discontinued after 100 had been built.

The successor to the Wirbelwind was the Ostwind. It carried the more effective 37mm flak gun in a fully rotating covered turret, but the end of the war was now in sight and only 43 machines were made to combat an Allied air force which was flying 20,000 aircraft in the skies over Germany.

Despite the revolutionary quality of many of the machines produced for Hitler's armies, they could never hope to match the sheer weight of numbers ranged against them.

This virtually complete air supremacy was put to extremely good use during the battle for Normandy. Allied bombers could reduce German beach defences, and cut German lines of communication, thus paralysing the build up of German forces opposite the amphibious and airborne landed British and American forces. And of course tactical air support could create absolute havoc to any German unit in Normandy foolish enough to try to move its strength by day. Newsreels of the period show German vehicles covered in branches in an attempt to disguise any vehicle movements from the air. The crew constantly scanned the horizon for the first signs of the British fighter-bombers, which made any movement on the ground an extremely hazardous undertaking.

MEDIUM TANKS IN NORMANDY

The US Handbook, as always, gave a good assessment of the armour types which the Allies were liable to meet on the ground in Normandy. By now the Allied intelligence network had a clear picture of the main machines in operation by the Wehrmacht forces and was able to produce a highly prescient insight into the Panzer forces in the field under very short timescales. This extract gives an assessment of the Medium and Heavy Tanks in service against the Allies during the 1944-45 period:

"Pz. Kpfw. IV.
Of the four tank types with which the Germans started the war, only the PZ. Kpfw. IV survives in service, although its role has been changed and it now carries a main armament which resembles the original gun only in calibre. It was armed originally with a short-barrelled 75mm gun (7.5cm Kw.K. (L/24)) and a machine gun mounted coaxially in the turret. In later models a hull machine gun was added. With this short, low-velocity gun the tank was primarily a close-support weapon. In 1942 it was re-armed with a long-barrelled, high velocity gun, the 7.5cm Kw.K. 40 (L/43), and thus changed its role from a close-support vehicle to a fighting tank and displaced the Pz. Kpfw. III as the main armament of the Panzer regiment. At the present time the Pz. Kpfw. IV is only a stopgap for the Panther. If enough Panther tanks become available, the disappearance of the Pz. Kpfw. IV may be expected.

The latest version of this tank to appear is the Model H, which differs from the Model G, of which details given, only in its 75mm gun being 48 calibres long instead of 43. There is no change in the ballistic characteristics.

This tank also has appeared in a commander's model, as an observation-post tank, as an ammunition tank, and as an armoured anti-aircraft vehicle. The hull and suspension also have been employed for self-propelled guns.

HEAVY TANKS

"Pz. Kpfw. PANTHER

In this tank, probably the most successful they have produced, the Germans have departed from their customary lines and sought inspiration in the design of the Russian T-34. The tank weighs about 50 short tons, and the effectiveness of its armour is enhanced by the fact that most of the plates are sloping. It has powerful armament, and has a high-powered engine which gives it a maximum speed of about 30 miles per hour. Internally the Panther is arranged in the standard German manner, with the driver's compartment in front, the fighting compartment in the centre section, and the engine at the rear.

"The Panther's design employs the double torsion-bar suspension. There are eight double, interleaved, large Christie-type bogie wheels. Each set of bogie wheels is mounted on a radius arm on the projecting end of a torsion bar which is coupled in series to a second one lying parallel to it. This ingenious device has the effect of doubling the length of the torsion bars.

"The Panther first was met in action on the Russian front in the summer of 1943. Originally designated Pz. Kpfw. V, its nickname, Panther, was

A Marder tank-destroyer moving past the flaming wreckage of a Russian village. The Marder was very much a stop-gap solution but it was widely used on the Eastern Front.

adopted as its official nomenclature in February 1944. The latest version to appear is the Model G. The principal reasons for the success of the Panther are its relatively high speed, manoeuvrability, dangerous armament, and good protection. Variants of the Panther tank which have been identified are the commander's version, the wrecker tank (Bergepanther) and the self-propelled gun Jagdpanther, which consists of the 8.8cm Pak 43/3 or 4 on the Panther chassis.

Pz. Kpfw. TIGER, MODEL B (KING TIGER)

This tank is a development of the Tiger along the lines of the Panther and with a new main armament, the 8.8cm Kw.K. 43 (L/71). The armour is as thick as that of the Tiger - in some parts thicker - and the improved design and the slope given to the majority of the plates (as in the Panther) give the tank vastly improved protection.

"The King Tiger is a tank designed essentially for defensive warfare or for breaking through strong lines of defence. It is unsuitable for rapid manoeuvre and highly mobile warfare because of its great weight and low speed. To accommodate the gun, the turret has been made unusually long in proportion to the total length of the tank. When 'buttoned up' the tank is extremely blind, and this is one of its weakest points.

"Since the King Tiger first appeared in August 1944 in Normandy, modifications have been made in the turret to eliminate the excessive plate bending involved in the original construction. The King Tiger virtually is invulnerable to frontal attack, but the flanks, which are less well protected, can be penetrated by Allied anti-tank weapons at most normal combat ranges."

After the war Fritz Bayerlein and the commander of the Panzer Lehr Division recorded the effects of the Allied air attacks. General Bayerlein, like all the other divisional commanders on the ground, knew that in the face of Allied air superiority it was almost suicidal to move during the day. Nonetheless, in their desire to rush as many troops into battle as quickly as possible the German High Command proved to be stubbornly inflexible, as Bayerlein bitterly recalled:

"At 2 o'clock in the morning of 6th June I was alerted that the invasion fleet was coming across the Channel. I was told to begin moving north that afternoon at 5 o'clock. Well this was too early. Air attacks had been severe in the daylight and everyone knew that everything that could fly would support the invasion. My request for a delay until twilight was refused. So we moved as ordered and immediately came under Allied air attack. I lost 20 or 30 vehicles by nightfall. At daylight next morning, the commander of 7th Army gave me a direct order to proceed and there was nothing else I could do, so the vehicles moved off as ordered. By the end of the day I had lost 40 trucks and 90 others. Five of my tanks were knocked out and 84 half-tracks, prime movers and self-propelled guns. These were serious losses for a Division not yet in action".

THE CHAIN OF COMMAND

On the German side, the Allied air superiority was just one of a number of serious disadvantages which had to be overcome if they were to conduct a successful campaign in the West. Chief among these was the confusion and disorganisation which prevailed in the chain of command. As Supreme Commander, Adolf Hitler constantly dabbled in every aspect of the forces at his command and he had a habit of reserving particularly powerful formations for his personal control.

The situation in France was an especially complicated one. The nominal Commander-In-Chief was von Runstedt, who controlled Army Group B, responsible for northern France and Belgium, and Army Group G, which was responsible for southern France, but Rommel, in command of Army Group B, enjoyed the favour of Hitler and in practice could not be overruled by his superiors. To further compound matters three of the Panzer Divisions operating within Rommel's area of influence were allocated to a separate formation known as Panzer Group West. This powerful grouping was designated as an Army Reserve and could only be deployed on the express authority of Hitler himself. This complicated and divisive policy was a result of Hitler's mistrust of the generals, and there is a great deal of evidence to suggest that the 'divide and rule' policy was a deliberate stratagem on Hitler's part.

By 1944 the flaws which affected the High Command were also reflected in the declining quality of the men in the ranks. The steady war of attrition in Russia meant that the Wehrmacht had to accept lower and lower standards of physical fitness for new recruits. Men who would previously have been refused for the armed services had to be called into action. One famous example is 'the stomach battalion' which was filled with middle-aged men who had stomach complaints, and therefore required a special diet.

At the other end of the spectrum from the ageing warriors of the stomach battalion, the German Army also had to allow the deployment of the 12th SS Panzer Division, better known as the Hitler Youth Division. This Division was led by experienced officers drawn from the famous SS Leibstandarte Division, and the ranks were filled almost entirely by teenagers. The average age of the Division was just 18. Although the

The gun-loader of a Panzer IV closes the turret side hatch in preparation for moving into battle. These side hatches were recognised as a major design flaw which compromised the effectiveness of the turret armour.

Hitler Youth Division fought with enormous courage and ferocity in the coming battle, the mere fact that it was now necessary to deploy Divisions composed of schoolboys shows the desperation of the German Army.

The overwhelming demands of a war on three fronts posed hosts of additional problems for the German logistics and supply system. Allied fighters and fighter-bombers had not restricted their attacks to the troops on the ground, they also carried out a massive air and interdiction campaign against the German supply lines. Roads and railway lines were mercilessly targeted, which meant that supplies of essential fuel and ammunition stocks could not reach the hard-pressed front line. By this stage of the war, Germany was under constant attack by Allied bomber formations and fuel was already in very short supply. In Normandy in many cases, German tanks, which were needed urgently to resist the invasion, could not move through lack of fuel.

To offset the many disadvantages which faced the German troops fighting on the ground in Normandy, they did enjoy some real advantages over the Allies. Many of the Panzer Divisions which would be used to fight the Allies had a strong core of battle hardened, experienced troops, who had already seen four years of brutal warfare. This gave them the mental toughness which would serve them in great stead during the coming battle.

The German forces also enjoyed a very real superiority in the quality of their tank forces. Not only were the crews hugely experienced thanks to their years on the Russian front, but the tanks themselves were far better than those used by the Allies. In particular the Tiger, Panther and the new King Tiger tanks could all engage Allied tanks at much longer ranges than those at which the Allies could fight back. The superior armour of the tanks also gave the Germans a marked advantage in battle. Time and time again, Allied tank soldiers described that disheartening experience of seeing their own shells bounce off the armour of the German tanks. This disparity in quality was to have a very real impact on the coming battles.

WITTMANN MOVES WEST

Wittmann also took advantage of this brief pause from the fighting, while he recovered, to marry his sweetheart, Hildegard Burmeister. Once again, it was an unmistakably Nazi event. After the wedding ceremony, performed by the civil magistrate, Wittmann accepted a gift copy of Mein Kampf, a speech was then given by SS-Sturmbannführer Pein, who declared that the philosophy of life of the Teutons still had meaning in their lives.

Wittmann's period of calm was to prove short-lived. On 6th June 1944 the Allies landed in Normandy. It was here that he would gain lasting fame.

The actual events of the D-Day landings themselves have little impact on our story, save to say that most of the Allied objectives were achieved on that crucial first day with one major exception - the capture of Caen. The only German armoured formation to be engaged against the Allies on 6th June was the 21st Panzer Division. As we have seen, this was not the famous formation which had fought so tenaciously under Rommel in North Africa. Now once again under his command, this reconstituted formation consisted of a tiny cadre of staff who had somehow escaped the North African debacle bolstered by a large number of inexperienced recruits.

The 21st Panzer Division fielded Panzer IVs as its main battle tanks, but it was also forced to use a number of captured French tanks which had been taken in 1940. Not surprisingly this was a less than fearsome adversary. Nonetheless, the 21st Panzer Division did enjoy some success on D-Day and actually managed to reach the Channel coast before being forced to withdraw by the arrival of superior Allied forces.

The city of Caen, which should have been in Allied hands on D-Day plus one, was to remain in German hands until 18th July, six weeks after the beginning of the battle. The reasons for the successful defence at Caen lay in the extremely difficult nature of the Bocage country in which the campaign was fought. The Bocage was a closely packed area of narrow lanes and high-banked hedgerows enclosing small fields and sunken lanes. It proved to be ideal defensive terrain where anti-tank guns and machine-gun nests could be concealed until the last possible moment.

The Allies had the advantage in numbers of tanks, but in the claustrophobic world of the Bocage, anti-tank teams could get close enough to the tanks to

With the Allied domination of the air, a number of attempts were made to produce decoys - in this case a wooden model of a Panther tank has been constructed.

attack them at murderously close range.

Faced with their inability to take the remaining D-Day objective the British High Command had no alternative to fighting in the Bocage. As casualties steadily mounted, the airfield at Carpiquet on the outskirts of Caen became a vital target. It was tenaciously defended by the youngsters of the Hitler Youth Division against a series of assaults by larger British forces.

These youngsters were disdainful of the traditions of the established SS Divisions of the German Army and for their divisional symbol they adopted a German runic symbol, but arrogantly placed it over the key symbol of the veteran SS Leibstandarte Division, in a challenge to the experienced members of the most senior SS Division, who now knew that they had a younger rival for the mantle of the Third Reich's leading fighting formation. The Hitler Youth Division performed very well in battle but the High Command must have taken a dim view of their habit of painting their girlfriend's names on their tanks in preference to the approved divisional numbering. Under incredibly difficult circumstances, the Hitler Youth Division fought so well that their commanders had little choice but to turn a blind eye to this breach of regulations.

VILLERS-BOCAGE

In an attempt to outflank these stubborn defenders at Carpiquet, Montgomery dispatched his highly experienced 7th Armoured Division, the 'Desert Rats', to make a broad sweep south of Caen, which was scheduled to begin on 12th June. The attack was aimed at the small town of Villers-Bocage and it was here that one of the most famous tank actions of the war would be fought. The Allied spearhead was halted and almost single-handedly destroyed in a fierce battle through the streets and fields surrounding Villers-Bocage by German Tiger tanks of 101st Heavy Battalion, led by the famous Michael Wittmann.

On the morning of 13th June 1944 Wittmann was near Villers-Bocage when he surprised a squadron of the County of London Yeomanry. The unsuspecting British troops had stopped for breakfast, when Wittmann's Tiger roared up. In no time the lightning reflexes of Wittmann and Bobby Woll had claimed twelve half-tracks, three light tanks and six medium tanks. Wittmann then dashed back and gathered three other Tigers and a Panzer IV.

At eight o'clock a lookout reported to SS-Obersturmführer Wittmann that a large column of enemy tanks was advancing on the Caen-Villers-Bocage road. Wittmann, who was in cover with his Tiger south of the road, saw a British armoured battalion followed by an English armoured troop carrier battalion advancing for Villers-Bocage.

This situation called for immediate action. Wittmann was unable to get the order to his other tanks, who had moved off. Instead, he immediately drove at the English column with his single tank, firing on the move. This rapid intervention initially split the column. For 80 metres Wittmann destroyed four Sherman Firefly tanks, positioning his Tiger next to the column and drove ten to thirty metres beside it firing in his direction of travel, along the column. He succeeded in knocking out 12 enemy tanks in a very short time. The accompanying battalion in armoured troop carriers, was almost completely wiped out. The following German tanks and infantry company took about 130 prisoners, but Wittmann drove on in advance of his company, into the town of Villers-Bocage.

Just before the Hotel du Bras d'Or he destroyed another Sherman then found himself facing several enemy tanks at the exit from the town, the Jeanne d'Arc Square. He subsequently turned his Tiger around and drove back down the main street. As it passed the Huet-Godefroy clothing store, the Tiger was hit by a shell fired by an anti-tank gun, which wrecked one of the drive sprockets.

TANKS IN BUILT-UP AREAS

Wittmann should have known better than to take a tank into the streets of the town. Despite the myriad dangers, the tank was the Queen of the battlefield in the wide-open spaces of North Africa and Russia. In the first four months of the war, the Germans discovered that there was one environment in which tanks should never be deployed - the built-up areas of towns and cities. There, they became especially vulnerable to lurking infantry and anti-tank guns.

The Germans learned this lesson as early as the Polish campaign of 1939, in the battle for Warsaw, but despite all of their previous experiences, these mistakes were repeated at Stalingrad, Kursk and in Normandy. Some commanders continued to commit tanks in towns right up to 1945.

In 1944 destroyed German tanks littered the streets of Villers-Bocage.

They were destroyed by concealed British anti-tank guns when they grew too confident and rolled into the town after a period of conspicuous success in the open fields around the town.

OPERATION EPSOM

During the last three weeks of June, as British casualties climbed, Montgomery knew that something had to be done to break the stalemate around Caen. His answer was Operation Epsom, which was launched on 26th June 1944. It began with a massive Allied artillery bombardment which pounded the enemy defences around the airfield. On the receiving end were units from three Panzer Divisions, the Hitler Youth Division who were still holding out around Carpiquet airfield, the 21st Division, and the elite Panzer Lehr Division. Despite the incredible bombardments these three Divisions held their ground and the 15th Scottish Infantry Division was badly mauled in the fighting. The Epsom offensive ground to a halt less than four miles from the British start line. But there was even worse to come. Anticipating German reinforcements, Lieutenant General Sir Miles Dempsey, Commander of the British Second Army, withdrew from even the small gains which had been achieved.

Operation Epsom was abandoned with Caen still in German hands, and with its failure Montgomery decided that it was now time to take a sledgehammer to Caen, which was to be attacked and captured in a frontal assault, codenamed Operation Charnwood, scheduled for 8th July. Until the Allies could break out past Caen, the beachhead would continue to be jammed with men and supplies, unable to move inland and highly vulnerable to counter-attack.

More importantly, the British had yet to capture an airfield. Charnwood was meant to provide a quick and brutal solution to the problems, but the sheer scale of the operation and the overwhelming level of back-up support available to Montgomery actually worked against the British forces.

To soften up the German defenders, no less than 467 British and Canadian bombers were allocated to attack the town prior to the offensive. This total disregard for the lives of their civilian Allies caused 10,000 civilian casualties. More importantly, it created a wilderness of rubble similar to that which had appeared after the Allied bombing at Monte Cassino in 1943. The huge bomb craters and acres of rubble produced a ready-made series of impenetrable defences. For the men who had seen action in Russia and Italy, the ruins of Caen provided a heaven-sent opportunity for men who knew from bitter experience exactly how to defend ruined cities.

Once again the attack had to be called off in the face of huge British casualties, but this time there was at least one glimmerr of consolation: the Royal Winnipeg Rifles had finally succeeded in capturing the airstrip at Carpiquet and wresting the garrison from the Hitler Youth Division.

Despite this moderate success, Montgomery was now the recipient of some worrying news from London. The enormous casualty rate around Caen was draining away the British replacements and if the loss rate continued at its present level replacements would run out at the end of July.

It was against this background that Montgomery decided to try one last offensive. Designed to capture the territory south of Caen, it was codenamed Operation Goodwood and scheduled for 17th July. Operation Goodwood was a massive tank attack involving all four British and Canadian Corps in Normandy. There were so many troops involved that there was a day's delay while all the necessary men and vehicles were brought into position. But hopes ran high that the war of attrition had finally turned in the British favour.

Goodwood began with an overwhelming air, naval and artillery bombardment, designed in blast a path for 750 tanks to advance towards the high ground south of Caen. Once again their opponents were to be men of the 1st SS Panzer Division, many of whom had been in action since 8th June. In the steady war of attrition the SS Corps had been reduced to a strength of just 100 tanks, but they could still command the deep defensive positions of the Bocage and they were backed up with the deadly 88mm anti-tank guns. The opening Allied barrage was so intensive it was described by some German veterans as the biggest and most intense artillery bombardment they had ever witnessed, even in Russia. There are accounts of Tiger tanks being thrown into the air. Under this intense storm of steel men went mad and had to be committed in mental hospitals, and there are at least two documented cases of German soldiers who committed suicide rather than endure the bombardment any longer.

Despite massive preparations which were made, Goodwood was an even greater failure than the previous offensives. Although the southern sector of Caen was cleared of the enemy, the Allies lost 200 tanks in a single day as they tried to cross the Orne. Fighting for Caen continued until 20th July but once again the operation had to be postponed, with part of the city still in German hands.

Despite all the British had done, Operation Cobra - the breakout from Normandy still faced some tough fighting before the American forces were finally able to break out of the Bocage and sweep southwards into open country. As the American offensive began to gather pace, the British forces took advantage of the confusion in the German ranks to form the northern pincer in this huge encircling movement, designed to trap the German forces in Normandy in a huge pocket centred on the town of Falaise.

As always the 1st SS Panzer Corps continued to resist every step of the way and they inflicted a severe reverse on the 1st Polish Armoured Division on 9th August when the Poles lost 150 tanks. Losses on this scale would have been catastrophic for the German forces, but to the Allies, with their resources, they appeared to be little more than an inconvenience. In the face of continued resistance the British forces kept up the drive southwards and by 20th August they had linked up with the American forces to close a ring around Falaise.

Although 40,000 German troops had managed to escape before the pocket was closed, 60,000 remained trapped inside along with the bulk of the German armour. It was now that the Allied air force swept in for the kill. Led by squadron after squadron of rocket-firing Typhoons, they pounded the densely packed columns of German troops as they struggled to free themselves from the Allied trap. The scene of carnage in the retreating columns is almost impossible to describe, 10,000 Germans died in the incessant air attacks; 50,000 more were taken prisoner.

These men represented the remains of 40 German Divisions which had been destroyed in the battle for Normandy. Four-fifths of the German Army who had been committed to the campaign in Normandy had been destroyed. Montgomery had won his battle, and exactly as planned, the Allies were on the River Seine by D-Day plus 90.

PANZERS IN THE FIELD

As the war continued each surviving tank in the German Panzer Divisions became an increasingly valuable asset. As battlefield losses rose, the war-ravaged German factories which were being pounded day and night by Allied bombers could no longer keep increasing the supply of war vehicles to match those destroyed.

However, provided it wasn't actually blown apart, or completely gutted by fire, a battle-damaged tank could actually be repaired and brought back into service.

For the Allies, with their limitless supplies of men and material, this was a less pressing issue, but for the Germans it was a vital matter. It was a source of great frustration to many German tank crews that Hitler himself placed a priority on the production of new tanks over the supply of replacement parts and engines. In many cases, old tanks could easily have been brought back into service at the from line with a regular supply of spare parts and engines, which would have been easier and more efficient.

OPERATIONAL STATUS OF TIGERS ON THE EASTERN AND WESTERN FRONTS

1ST SEPT. 1942 - 5TH APRIL 1945

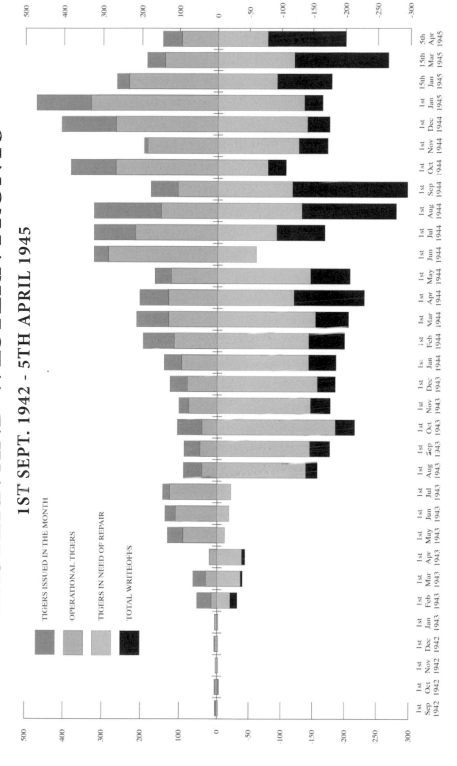

TIGERS ISSUED IN THE MONTH

OPERATIONAL TIGERS

TIGERS IN NEED OF REPAIR

TOTAL WRITEOFFS

Tiger II's of Schwere Heeres Panzer Abteilung 503 (s.H.Pz.Abt. 503) 'Feldherrnhalle' posing in formation for the German newsreel.

PANZERKAMPFWAGEN VI (B)
SD.KFZ. 182

The Tiger II Ausf B was known as the King Tiger ("Konigstiger" / VK 4503 (H)) and is recognized as the most powerful combat tank of the war. It resembled the Panther more than the Tiger I and had a long barrelled 88mm gun which could destroy a Sherman Tank at a range of 2000 metres. Like the Tiger I, the Tiger II suffered from poor mobility from its excessive weight and high fuel consumption.

Production of the King Tiger began in January 1944 after Hitler had passed the wooden mock-ups presented to him the previous October. The crew of five were protected by a thick sloping body of armour which very few weapons could hope to defeat. The King Tiger was compared favourably with the Russian T-34/85 and JS-II and had a reputation as a superior war machine.

Tiger IIs take shelter under trees to avoid being seen by Allied aircraft during the fighting in the Normandy campaign.

Pz. Kpfw. VI Tiger II Ausf B

Armour - Type: Homogenous rolled / welded nickel-steel

Hull Front : 100 - 150mm	Hull Top: 40mm	Turret Sides: 80mm
Hull Sides: 80mm	Hull Bottom: 25 - 40mm	Turret Rear: 80mm
Hull Rear: 80mm	Turret Front: 180mm	Turret Top: 40mm

Armament

Main Armament: 8.8cm L/71 KwK43	Secondary Armament: 2 x 7.92mm MG34	Ancillary Armament: Grenade / Bomb Launcher

Engine - Maybach HL230 P30 V-12 Water-cooled petrol

Crew	5	Max. Vertical Obstacle	0.85 m
Hull Length	7.25 m	Suspension Type	Torsion Bar
Length (gun forward)	10.43 m	Capacity	231 (5 gallons)
Width	3.72 m	Output	700bhp/515kW at 3000rpm
Overall Height	3.72 m	Power / Weight Ratio	10 bhp/tonne
Gross Weight	68.5 tonnes	Fuel Capacity	8601 (189 gallons)
Ground Pressure	0.78kg/cm²	Range (Road)	170 km (105 miles)
Fording Capacity	1.6 m	Range (Crosscountry)	120 km (70 miles)
Max. Gradient	36°	Max. Speed	38 km/h (24 mph)
Max. Trench Width	2.5 m	Suspension Type	Torsion Bar

From November 1944 a number of Tiger IIs were converted to command tanks mounted with additional radio equipment. This was designated as the Befehlswagen Tiger II Ausf B.

The first time that the King Tiger went into combat was in May 1944 near Minsk, followed by Poland in July. It also saw battle on both the Western and Eastern Fronts and was an effective combat weapon. The problems with mobility presented by its huge weight, and the vast amount of precious production resources consumed by each King Tiger ultimately outweighed the advantages of the mark.

TANK NUMBERING

German tanks usually carried a three-figure identification number painted on the turret.

Regimental staffs usually used the letter R in place of the letter 0, so R01 would be the regimental commander. Battalion staffs used the number of the unit in Roman numerals, therefore T01 would be the commander of the 1st battalion. The first number specified the company, the second number specified the platoon number and the third number specified the number of the tank within the four tank section or (Zug). Using this system tank number 414 would be the fourth tank in the first Zug of the fourth company.

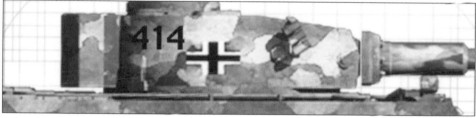

Headquarters command tanks in companies were identified by the prefix 0 followed by a designated number from 1-9.

Company command tanks were generally identified by the number 0 in place of the platoon number and a standard number which identifies the officer's place in the hierarchy. For example, number 004 for the HQ Leader and 005 for the Company Commander.

THE WESTERN FRONT
1944 - 1945

"The breakthrough along the entire front was to be carried out by the infantry Divisions. The armour was then to exploit the shock effect of the assault and drive through the gaps. It was to head due west into the enemy rear. It was to by-pass strongly held villages and not worry about exposed flanks. These tactics had frequently been employed with success in the East."

**GENERAL HASSO VON MANTEUFFEL,
ON THE ARDENNES OFFENSIVE**

By 17th September 1944 the Allies had liberated France, Belgium and Luxembourg and had reached Dutch and German by 1st September 1944. On 17th September 1944 they launched an ill-fated operation to gain a bridgehead across the lower Rhine, while outflanking the defences of the West Wall. Codenamed Market-Garden, this operation ended on 25th September as a partial failure because intelligence reports of the German strength in the area were ignored. The 9th and 10th SS Panzer Divisions therefore shared the dubious honour of contributing to Germany's last clear-cut victory in arms during the Second World War. Although unsuccessful, Operation Market-Garden provided the Allies with an important salient for the upcoming drive into Germany. On 16th December 1944 the Germans launched their Ardennes offensive, designed to split the Allied Armies and to capture the port city of Antwerp: although this offensive enjoyed some success at the early stage it was contained, and on 28th January 1945 the focus switched to the last battles in the East.

CAPTURED ALLIED TANKS

The Allied forces at this time were equipped with a variety of American, British and Canadian made armoured fighting vehicles, and the Germans captured relatively few of them, mainly as a result of local counter-attacks. By this point

The King Tiger was only available in very limited numbers during the fight in Normandy. This picture, taken in the late summer of 1944, shows one of the four machines which made it into the fighting.

Germans were either on the defensive or retreating eastwards.

The American M4 Sherman medium tank (and its variants) was the most numerous Allied tank following D-Day and the Germans knew it from North Africa, Italy and Russia. The M4 Sherman tank was designated by the Germans as Panzerkampfwagen M4 748(a): they captured a few vehicles which were then grouped into captured tank platoons and units in the west. These formations included the famous 21st Panzer Division, which was continually engaged against the Allies until early 1945, as well as the 25th Panzer Grenadier Division. The 10th SS Panzer Division 'Frundsberg', which was also engaged against the Allies until early 1945, had at least ten captured Sherman tanks, the 5th Fallschirmjager Division and Panzer Brigade 150 were also known to have used some captured Sherman tanks. SS Panzer Division 'Frundsberg' captured 12 Sherman tanks in the Upper Alsace (Western Germany) on 17th January 1945 and operated them against the Russians until 7th May 1945, when they were destroyed by their crews in the Schmiedeberg (now Kowary, Southern Poland). In addition to those units, there were a number of unrecorded tanks pressed into service by German units. SS-Obersturmbannführer Otto Skorzeny's Panzer Brigade 150 was to be equipped with ten Sherman tanks for the Ardennes offensive. When it was organised in November 1944, in practice only two unserviceable Sherman tanks were available along with two troop carriers, five to ten scout cars and some 15 to 30trucks. The 5th Fallschirmjager Division on the other hand utilised some six captured Sherman tanks as late as January 1945, following the Ardennes offensive. In July 1944 Schwere Panzer Abteilung 503 captured two British Sherman tanks near Colombelles. Schwere Panzerjäger Abteilung 654 is known also to have used a captured Sherman tank as a recovery vehicle in late 1944 and early 1945. During the fighting in Normandy, 1st SS Panzer Corps comprising the 1st SS Panzer Division 'Leibstandarte Adolf Hitler', the 12th SS 'Hitlerjugend' and the Panzer Lehr Division managed to capture a number of Allied tanks including at least one Sherman Firefly. This variant was armed with a British 17 pound gun mounted in a modified turret and was designated as Sherman VC (V - base variant and C -17 pound gun) Firefly. There are a number of photographs taken by Germans of captured Fireflies being examined and tested but it is unknown if any were

The tank hunter version of the King Tiger was due to be in action at the start of Operation Wacht am Rhein but to Hitler's dismay transport difficulties delayed the appearance of the machines in which he had a pathetically high expectation.

pressed into service, and if so it can only have been for a short period of time. A few Fireflies from 7th British Tank Division were captured following the engagement by the most successful and famous tank commander of World War II SS Hauptsturmführer Michael Wittmann, at Villers-Bocage.

In addition, German units captured a few M10 Wolverine tank destroyers in late 1944. At least one was captured by the 6th Panzer Division in Belgium in November 1944 and a few more were taken during the Ardennes offensive. They were temporarily pressed into service, their brief service lives limited to only a few days by the shortage of ammunition and fuel. They were designated by the Germans as Jagdpanzer M10(a).

A few M5 Stuart Light Tanks were also captured by the German units and temporarily engaged in 1944 under the designation of Panzererkampfwagen M3 740(a).

THE BRITISH TANKS

The British Cruiser Tank M.VIII Cromwell (A27M) was one of the most important tanks in British service during the campaign in the west. Its variants were armed with a 6-pound gun (75mm gun) and the 95mm howitzer and were operated by a crew of five. Only a few Cromwells were captured by the Germans and were designated as Kreuzer Panzerkampfwagen Mk.VIII(e). It appears that at least two machines from the 7th British Tank Division were captured following the engagement at Villers Bocage, including a Cromwell VI (armed with a 95mm howitzer) and a Cromwell with the 75mm gun. There is photographic evidence of them being either examined or tested, but if any were used it could only have been for a short time.

THE ARDENNES OFFENSIVE

After the German failure at Kursk, even Hitler at last began to realise that it was now impossible to inflict a serious defeat on the Russians. Despite all the evidence to the contrary, Hitler believed that a well executed offensive in the West could defeat the western Allies and free up much needed forces for the East, to try at least and halt the Russian advances. With his planned western offensive, he anticipated he could force the Allies to sue for peace from a stalemate position, but even Hitler must have known this was to be the last

A Jagpanzer IV utilised the excellent chassis of the Panzer IV and combined that reliability with an excellent 75mm gun and well sloped thick frontal armour to produce a highly efficient fighting vehicle.

chance for the Panzers.

One thing the Panzer Divisions did have on their side was experience, and before they were swept away, the small groups of Tigers performed heroically. Michael Wittmann alone was responsible for a huge number of Allied tank kills. By June 1944 Wittmann and his Tiger had been responsible for taking out more than 130 Russian tanks when he was transferred to the Western Front. Even with the skills of men like these, the Tigers were still being destroyed as fast as they were being delivered, and Wittmann himself fell in action in August 1944, his machine totally destroyed. Such losses were simply unsustainable.

In 1944, despite the pressures of Allied bombing raids, some 20,000 German armoured fighting vehicles were manufactured. But battlefield losses were running at some 23,000 machines, so the number of German tanks available in 1944 at the front line actually fell.

During 1944, on average, there were never more than 100 Tigers available for action at any given time on the whole of the Russian Front. The remaining machines were either under short or long-term repair. It was this tiny force which forged a legend.

On the Western Front the Allies by now enjoyed total air supremacy, and the Allied air force was able to rove at will, destroying German aircraft on the ground.

The high rate of attrition on their armoured force caused the Germans to cast around desperately for a solution. One successful expedient was to dispense with the turret of the new Panther tanks to produce turret less vehicles with less flexibility but heavier firepower. They were also easier and quicker to manufacture; three could be made for every two tanks.

These tank killers were known by the German name Jagdpanther. By this stage of the war German armour was fighting almost exclusively defensive battles for which the Jagdpanthers were perfectly suited. They could lie in wait, firing from fixed positions.

As with the turret-less tanks, there was also a steady increase in size and armament in the tank hunters, which evolved from the simple Marder I, based on the Panzer I, to the ultimate tank killing machine, the Jagdtiger, based on the upgraded Tiger II. Massive armour and a superb high calibre gun made these machines deadly. But, once again, the design and engineering effort took valuable resources away from producing simpler designs in the volume the Germans needed.

PREPARING THE ASSAULT

By a small miracle of logistics the hard-pressed Germans of the Third Reich somehow managed to scrape together the men and machines for one last great offensive. In the middle of December 1944 Hitler launched his surprise winter

The desperate plan for the Ardennes offensive called for the employment of captured American vehicles. With the failure of the forces on the ground to deliver enough machines, Kommando Skorzeny who was to use the captured tanks had to resort to attempting to disguise German tanks as Allied vehicles.

offensive in the Ardennes region of Belgium. For this offensive 250,000 men and over 1,000 tanks and armoured vehicles had somehow been assembled.

After the destructive battles through France in the summer, this force represented the very last reserves of manpower. Hitler placed all of his hopes on this offensive, the last great offensive in the west during the Second World War.

The plan for this attack was fairly straightforward. The Ardennes region had provided a successful launch pad for the Blitzkreig campaigns of 1940. Once again Hitler planned to push a strong, armoured-led thrust through the Allied held positions and on to Antwerp. This would split the two main Allied Armies and, he hoped, force them to accept defeat or evacuate back to England as they had done in 1940.

Unlike 1940, however, the Germans were fighting an Army who were used to their tactics. This time the Allies had better equipped forces that they could call upon to meet any threat. The terrain and supply problems did not favour the Germans this time either. The German Generals could see the shortcomings of the offensive, but at this late stage in the war few of them dared to question Hitler's authority for fear of their lives.

The Germans had been busy developing new tanks and assault gun designs during this period. In 1944, during the battle, the Allies captured the powerful monster known as the Sturmmoser or Sturm Tiger. The troops who knocked out this giant adversary must have breathed a huge sigh of relief, because this devastating machine was so powerfully armed it had outgrown mere artillery power and was equipped with a rocket launcher of ferocious attacking force.

It was designed to attack even the strongest fortification. Due to the range limitations of its rocket launcher, the Sturm Tiger had to get very close to its target to fire its payload, but it was so heavily armoured that it was nearly impervious to any anti-tank gun on the battlefield. The Sturm Tiger's role was to rumble right up to infantry bunkers or strong points and fire the rocket almost at point blank range. Obviously, the chances of survival for its target were slim indeed.

The enormous rockets it carried were so heavy the vehicle needed its own crane to be able to load the shells. Once loaded, the inside of the tank was so cramped it carried enough rounds for only thirteen shots, but when it did fire, the results were devastating.

The Sturm Tiger was the last in a line of turret less tanks which the German Army had produced in increasing quantities since the outbreak of the Second World War, but this highly specialised vehicle was produced so late in the war that only 19 were manufactured before Germany finally surrendered. One of the most significant new designs was the Tiger II B, or King Tiger.

The Tiger II is a remarkable tank by any standards. It mounted a bigger and more powerful gun than the Tiger I and the armour was thicker and sloped, giving it a tremendous advantage. For a tank which came into service in 1944, it looks almost good enough to use today, and was a considerable tribute to the German designers. The trouble was that it was getting near the limit of weight that the engine and transmission could stand and, of course, producing a tank like this under wartime conditions was a tremendous strain, especially when the industry was being heavily bombed. Therefore, in terms of gun power and armour, it outclassed tanks such as the T-34, but was never available in sufficient numbers and certainly wasn't easy to ship around the country in a hurry and get to trouble spots, so it has to be regarded as a failure in terms of tank design.

The Tiger B was the largest practical tank to see action in the Panzer Division. Already its huge size was giving enormous difficulty in negotiating narrow roads and moving across bridges, few of which could carry its huge weight. It also needed huge stocks of the vital fuel supplies which Germany could no longer provide.

Around 50 vehicles were fitted with Porsche turrets, the remaining 439 Tiger IIs were fitted with the Henschell turret. The first time that the King Tigers saw action was during the Allied invasion France in June 1944; around 15 King Tigers were involved in these battles. A full battalion of 45 King Tigers was later sent to the Arnhem area in September 1944, where they helped to ensure that the Allied Operation Market-Garden was thwarted. They were next to feature in the coming German offensive in the Ardennes. Like the Tiger I, this tank was better suited to the open country and the majority of them were sent east to battle with the advancing Russians. A full battalion of 45 tanks was earmarked for the assault. The SS 501st heavy tank battalion, which was part of the 6th Panzer Army, was placed with Kampfgruppe Peiper, at the front of the armoured advance.

By late 1944 the assault guns and tank destroyers had become a valuable addition to the German arsenal. The Jagdtiger was a highly effective tank destroyer but a total of only 70 Tiger II chassis were ever converted to the new design. This was enough to equip two heavy tank destroyer units. One of these, the 653rd, saw action during the Ardennes offensive. This very imposing machine was more suited to the open country and not the closed confines of the Ardennes. Overall, this vehicle was an excellent destroyer of Allied tanks, but its introduction was too late in the war and the numbers too few to have any effect on the final outcome.

The manufacture of assault guns was more cost effective and these types increasingly proved their worth on the battlefield. More and more resources were put into developing tank designs and the trend was not always to larger machines. One of these new designs was the Hetzer, based on the vehicle chassis of the 38(t).

Another assault gun design used by the Germans during the Ardennes offensive was the JagdPanzer IV Lang. This vehicle was based on the Panzer IV chassis and weighed around 26 tons. The crew contained four men. Its main armament was the very potent 75mm L/70 main gun; this was the same gun that was used on the Panther. One MG42 machine gun provided the close quarter support. The armour protection was 80mm thick and the top speed was 24mph. This vehicle had a low silhouette and, together with the very effective main gun, became a very capable killer as the US handbook made clear:

"Jagdpanther, 8.8cm Pak 4313 OR 43,14 (L/71) ON THE PANTHER CHASSIS. (I) General. This tank destroyer is intended for engaging armoured targets at long ranges from stationary positions. A single, heavy, sloping plate protects the front of both hull and superstructure. The gun is mounted centrally in this plate, giving the vehicle the appearance of an assault-gun, with the gun rather high."

These new tank designs joined the existing German machines including the Panzer IV, Panther and Tiger. On the whole the German tanks were probably superior to those of the Allies, who still relied on the Sherman.

'WACHT AM RHEIN'

The Ardennes offensive was given the code name 'Wacht am Rhein' or 'Watch on the Rhine.' Hitler, however, did not fully realise the extent to which the situation in December 1944 was very different to that in May 1940.

For one, the planned route for the new offensive cut straight across the Ardennes. In 1940 the route used had travelled in a southwesterly direction and utilised the road system that generally ran in that direction also. The new route was to northwest and the Ardennes offered few northwesterly roads. This would seriously restrict movement of the German forces and cause immense delays in the deployment of the vital armoured spearheads.

Another restrictive feature of the planning was the lack of sufficient fuel. To make up for this, the German troops were expected to capture enemy fuel dumps and supplies en route. Even the amount of fuel that was originally requested for the start of the operation could not be fulfilled. The fuel tractor on its own was to play a significant part in the eventual failure of the operation. The deployment of the forces was not best suited to ensure success either. The advance towards Antwerp required the forces to swing northeast after the Germans had reached the Meuse river. Given that the Allies had strong forces in Belgium and Holland, it was suspected that they would eventually mount a counter-attack into the German left flank. However, the strongest armoured German forces were situated on the right flank and too far removed to meet any potential threat.

The Germans did have some elements in their favour. The weather was bad at this time and it was expected to remain like this for at least a week. The overwhelming Allied superiority in the air had inflicted heavy losses on the Germans over the last few months. The much-feared Jabos or rocket-firing planes struck fear into the heart of every German soldier. The poor weather situation prevalent in the middle of December 1944 would keep the Allied planes on the ground for the vital opening phases of the attack. This would, with luck, allow the advance to make a good start and reach some of the objectives.

When the attack began, the scale of the unleashed German forces surprised the Allied commanders. Some of them had expected a German attack imminently, but not to this extent. Some of the forces that were part of the German attack had been severely mauled during the Normandy battles. The planned area of attack was also being held by Allied troops who themselves had only recently been involved in heavy fighting around the Hurtgen forest. Hitler was confident of success and did not allow any alterations to his plans. By 16th December everything was in place. The quiet Ardennes sector was about to erupt with the sounds of battle. The Panzers were once again moving west.

The Germans had assembled an impressive line up of tank forces for the offensive. The powerful 6th Panzer Army were positioned in the north under Obergruppenführer 'Sepp' Dietrich. This force included the 1st SS Paneer Division 'Leibstandarte Adolf Hitler', 2nd SS Panzer Division 'Das Reich', 9th SS Hitler Panzer Division 'Hohenstaufen' and the 12th SS Panzer Divisions. Their task was to advance along the route from their forming-up area near Dahlem in Germany and into Belgium around the town of Losheim. Their objective was to cross the Meuse just below Liege and advance onto Antwerp.

Just to the south of this force was the 5th Panzer Army under the command of Lieutenant General Hasso von Manteuffel. He had the 2nd Panzer, 9th Panzer, 116th Panzer and the Panzer 'Lehr' Divisions together with the

15th Panzer Grenadier Division. Their objective was to move from Prum in Germany and onto Antwerp via Brussels. The 7th Army under General Erich Bradenberger was to take the southernmost route into Luxembourg. This was an infantry-only formation made up from the 5th Infantry Divisions including a grounded Parachute Division. They were to move from Bitburg in Germany and into the area held by the US 3rd Army, with the objective of tying down these forces. All of these forces were part of Army Group B commanded by Field Marshal Model.

They had very limited reserves, in the shape of the 3rd Panzer Grenadier Division and the 'Führer Begleit' Brigade and the 'Führer' Grenadier Brigade.

This total force had 2,000 artillery pieces, over 1,000 tanks and assault guns and 250,000 men. To have assembled this impressive force after the destructive battles in Normandy and the east was an exceptional feat on its own but the size masked some real weakness. Each of the Panzer Armies relied on Volksgrenadier battalions to provide its infantry support. These men were Germany's equivalent of the British Home Guard. They were scraped together into formations which were intended as a last ditch defence mechanism: they had no part to play in a full-bloodied offensive.

Another view of one of the Panzer IV tanks disguised as an Allied vehicle for the Ardennes offensive.

The devastating combination of artillery fire and mastery of the skies meant that there were few hiding places for German tanks in the closing phase of the war.

The storm was about to break on just four Infantry Divisions who were part of the US V Corps under Major General Gerow. Two were positioned opposite the 6th Panzer Army. Facing Manteuffel in the centre were the 28th and 106th Infantry Divisions who were part of Major General Troy Middleton's VIII Corps. In the south facing Brandenberger's men were the 9th Armoured and the 4th Infantry Divisions. All of these American units had recently been involved in heavy fighting and were in the area for a rest. They totalled around 80,000 men, less than 450 tanks and assault guns and around 400 artillery pieces. Although initially outnumbered, the Allies had strong forces positioned close by, including Patton's 3rd Army, that could be called upon to back up the defences in this area.

On the morning of 16th December the German artillery opened fire along the entire front line. The object of this was to confuse the enemy, disrupt their lines of communication and open gaps in the lines. Due to the extreme secrecy, the Germans were unable to identify the Allied positions in advance. The result was that the German bombardment had limited success. It did sever Allied lines of communication, inflict some casualties and provide some confusion, but not to the extent that was hoped by the Germans. In the north,

Dietrich's forces advanced towards Elsenborn Ridge. A German parachute drop had been ordered for this area with the objective of capturing a vital road junction in the Baraque Michel. This drop did not go well as the Falschirmjäger were scattered over a wide area. They found themselves in amongst the US 1st Infantry Division, so the small force had to find their way back to their own lines. The failure of this small, but significant, action would delay the advance of the SS armour.

Dietrich's men had Obersturmbannführer Jochen Peiper at their head: this SS officer was a seasoned veteran of Russia and Normandy. He had a battalion of 45 King Tigers under his command, but in the opening stages they were not with the lead force. He helped to ensure that the advance got off to a good start towards the Elsenborn Ridge, under the cover of the bad weather. However, the Americans gave a good account of themselves and succeeded in preventing the Germans from taking this vital high ground. Slightly south of here the main body of the 1st SS Panzer Division moved into the gap that had been opened up between the US V and VIII Corps. The route of their advance was towards Honsfield, which they reached on the following day. Various delays had taken place, but by the end of day one progress had been made.

In the 5th Panzer Army's area the advance got off to a good start. They moved against the thinly spread American units and forced through the enemy positions. Some of the American forces slowed the advance and managed to hold some of the bridges in the area. By the end of day one, however, crossings had been made over the river Our and the German Panzers rolled on towards Clervaux. Further south the 7th Army ran into similar difficulties to Dietrich. The ground was favourable to the defender and Brandenberger's men made little headway.

Overall, although difficulties had been encountered, 17th December would see the all-important armour committed in strength. However, the American High Command was starting to react to the German attack, and reinforcements were being rushed to the area to meet the threat. Among these reinforcements were the 7th and 10th Armoured Divisions together with the 82nd and 101st Airborne Divisions. These last two units were ordered to the vital road junction of Bastogne. The German attempt to reach their objective continued. Dietrich in the north was keen to make progress. He moved the 12th SS Panzer Division from their attack on Elsenborn Ridge, and pushed them in behind the 1st SS Panzer Division who were moving towards the Ambleve River. The move actually helped to relieve the pressure on the Americans defending the ridge area, and to set up a defence that the Germans could not breach.

Dietrich had an ace up his sleeve in the shape of the 150th Panzer Brigade. This force was under the command of Otto Skorzeny (probably best known for his dramatic rescue of Mussolini). They were using captured American jeeps and trucks together with German tanks adapted to resemble American tank destroyers. Their task was to infiltrate behind the American lines and race ahead to capture vital crossings and hold them for the main forces. They were also to pass false information to the enemy and generally cause confusion. They did have some successes; the most notable was when they reached the Meuse. They were unable to capitalise on this success as the main body of troops was too far behind. Also, groups of them began to get stopped and arrested by the Americans. The rumours quickly spread that there were Germans driving around posing as friendly forces. Everyone became a suspect and some very high-ranking American officers found themselves in awkward situations. Eisenhower himself was confined to his headquarters in fear of assassination. Although their objectives were not entirely reached, the psychological effect that this unit had was very widespread and out of proportion to the small numbers involved. Most of those that were captured were shot as spies.

Peiper's advance in the north had come across a group of Americans who they took prisoner. They were held in a field near the crossroads at Malmedy and it was here that around eighty of them were shot. The Americans insisted this was in cold blood, the Germans claimed they were trying to escape. The bodies were found a short time later and the search went out for the culprits. The story spread throughout the American lines and actually helped to instil resistance in the men. Just before this incident, Peiper's men had succeeded in capturing a fuel dump at Bullingen, which had helped the advance to continue. They reached the bridge at Stavelot, but were held up for a number of hours when they came under attack.

The advance into Stavelot resumed the following morning and the town was captured. The advance continued towards Trois Fonts; close to here were the bridges that cross the Salm and Ambleve rivers. These bridges were destroyed by the American defenders as Peiper's men approached, and Peiper was forced to move back towards La Gleize. He tried to advance through to Chenaux, where another bridge crossed the Ambleve, but came under attack from American planes, so set up defences around La Gleize and Stoumont.

With the failure of this advance, the main emphasis was shifted to the 5th Panzer Army's sector. They were having better luck against the US 106th

New recruits are taken through their paces using the turret of a Panzer II for instruction. By this phase of the war training vehicles were in very short supply.

Division. However the US 101st Airborne Division had reached Bastogne and set up all round defences. They offered such stiff resistance that Manteuffel ordered his forces to bypass the town and continue their advance. This created a "bulge within a bulge" and would provide a very prickly thorn in the Germans' side. On 22nd December the Germans went to Bastogne with a white flag and the offer of surrender for the Americans. The garrison commander, General McAuliffe, offered his famous 'nuts' reply. The key town of St.Vith, further north, had fallen to the Germans on the same day. They had been fighting around this town for days, and as in

The next wave of tank men are shown here having completed the officer training part of the course. These are the men who would provide the tank commanders for the last two years of the war.

other areas these delays allowed the Americans to build up defences further back. On the 24th Manteuffel's forces reached an area just west of Celles. This was to become the furthest point reached by the Germans during this offensive. Christmas Day 1944 saw the besieged Bastogne coming under increasing pressure from the Germans. They pushed more and more forces into the area in an attempt to eliminate the pocket. Further south, elements of Patton's forces were moving closer and, on Boxing Day, they managed to force an opening through the German lines and into Bastogne. This was the start of the end of Hitler's Ardennes offensive.

Another significant occurrence around this time was the improvement in the weather. This allowed the Allies to send sorties against the German positions. At La Gleize, Peiper could see the hopelessness of the situation. His men were receiving a pounding by American artillery and tanks; the Americans fired over 58,000 shells into the area during the battle. This provides a good picture of the punishing fire that Peiper's men would have endured. He ordered that the tanks and half-tracks that had not already been destroyed by Allied fire be destroyed by his own men to prevent their use by the enemy. They were out of vital fuel and ammunition. He left some of his men behind to give the impression that they were still fighting and also to look after the 150 American prisoners they had captured. He took the remaining 800 survivors with him and made for German-held lines, which he managed to reach a few days later. The escape attempt had been dangerous and on more than one occasion his men became involved in fire fights with American forces that were moving across Peiper's escape route. Peiper not only left behind some of his men, he also left behind an impressive bag of irreplaceable vehicles that included six King Tigers, 13 Panthers, six Panzer IVs and over 50 other vehicles including around 45 armoured half-tracks. These losses were hard to take at this stage of the war.

Further south, the corridor into Bastogne was slowly widened. Ferocious battles took place around this area and both sides fought desperately for control. The Americans pushed more and more forces into the Bastogne area including the 4th Armoured Division, the 26th Infantry and the 80th Infantry Divisions. The 'Battle of the Bulge' as the Americans called the battle, was proving a very hard fight for both sides. As the Allies were able to push more forces into the area, they slowly succeeded in pushing the Germans back. By 2nd January 1945 the front line had been reduced by around fifteen kilometres.

Although the Ardennes offensive is always associated with American forces, British forces also played a vital role. In the early stages of the operation Montgomery had recognised the importance of the river Meuse to the Germans and had placed strong British forces in a defensive position along the northern sector. He was also given command of some of the American forces; this in itself caused a rift between the Allies and in some respects almost helped Hitler to achieve his goal. When the time was right, Montgomery launched a counter-attack into the German lines with the objective of linking with the Americans further south. This objective was finally reached on 4th January at the town of La Roche. This meant that a solid defensive line now existed that the Germans could not hope to penetrate. Also, the river Meuse, vital to German success, was now out of reach.

Hitler still ordered the advance to continue and achieve the original objective, but at this stage it was an increasingly impossible task. However, the intensity of the battle is best described by Patton himself, who on 6th January expressed his very real fears that the war could still be lost by the Allies.

The 1st SS Panzer Division were moved down to this area at the end of December to help destroy the Americans. This did nothing to change the final outcome and only added to the German casualty list.

Allied fighters flew sortie after sortie against the Germans and inflicted further aerial destruction on the increasingly pressurised German forces. The Luftwaffe launched their own attacks in the early days of January, when around a thousand planes flew against Allied targets. This attack had some notable successes, including the destruction of 300 Allied aircraft and the damage to some twenty-five Allied airfields. The Germans themselves lost around a hundred planes and, more importantly, experienced pilots. At the time the Allies played down this part of the battle. Towards the middle of January some of the German units were withdrawn, including the 1st SS Panzer Division, which put even more pressure on the remaining German forces. Hitler had also launched another smaller offensive called 'Nordwind' at the start of January. It had the objective of destroying the Allied positions around the Vosges Mountains. The attacks quickly bogged down against the Allied defenders, but the fighting continued until mid-January. The operation itself

A Pz.Kpfw VI (B) King Tiger tank knocked-out and abandoned by its crew during the latter stages of the fighting in Normandy.

achieved nothing of any significance, but it represented a high irreplaceable cost to the Germans in men and machines.

By the end of January the front line was back to where it had been at the start of the German offensive six weeks earlier. The cost to both sides was high; the Allies lost around 75,000 men, the Germans suffered around 120,000 casualties and lost a considerable number of irreplaceable tanks. As the Allies discovered when they came across the vehicles, a large portion of them had been abandoned because their fuel tanks had run dry. The Allies could make their losses good, but the Germans simply could not. The loss of the Ardennes offensive removed any reserves that the Germans possessed and which could have been used in the defence of the Reich. In the east the Russians had launched their new offensive in January 1945. There was nothing available to counter this threat. Hitler's last gamble in the west had failed completely and the end of the Third Reich was in sight.

An artist's impression of the problems of keeping the Sturmgeschütz re-supplied in action. The limited storage capacity meant that these precious machines had to be constantly re-stocked with ammunition, even under fire.

LAST BATTLES IN THE EAST

"There was much we could do but we were not magicians. There needs to be close co-operation between Panzers and the infantry. Often we came under the command of infantry officers who did not understand how Panzers should be handled in action. We lost many machines through carelessness and inexperience... heartbreaking."

OBERST PAUL 1946, ON THE BATTLE FOR BERLIN

After the failure of the Ardennes Offensive the writing was now on the wall for the men of the Panzerwaffe, but there was still more fighting to be done. Despite the deteriorating situation, Hitler now sought to rush his precious Panzer Divisions to Hungary where they were commanded to take part in Operation Spring Awakening to secure the liberation of Budapest and secure the Reich's last supply of oil.

The weight of numbers was now running very strongly against the Panzerwaffe; only the quality of the German armour now separated the two sides.

Although they were massively outnumbered, the diminishing ranks of German Panzers managed incredible feats in action.

There was also a number of far-sighted innovations which had to be rushed through to try to stem the tide. Amongst these radical leaps in technology was the introduction of night-vision equipment into the Panther tanks, which actually worked in practice. The inevitable teething problems and production difficulties meant that this development made little practical impact in the full, but the technology was developed for the future.

HERR RUEHS

One veteran of the Panther in action was Herr Ruehs who later recalled his experiences in the closing stages of the war:

"I had originally been a Panzer grenadier but I didn't want to sit outside the tanks anymore, so I trained as a medium-wave radio operator. Before this I was acting as a gun-loader. Our own gun-loader had got out to help tow another tank that had gone off the road and broken down - it had lost its right-hand caterpillar - they were fired at, and he was badly wounded.

"We went into action at the railway embankment near the Plattensee. We couldn't get any further unfortunately although we had ten good, almost new, Panther tanks. The road was occupied by a PAK, and they were able to see us very well so we just couldn't advance any further. We had our first casualty there. As soon as we left the road with our heavy tanks, one was hit and it blew up. They were all killed inside the tank of course.

"My best friend was also killed there. He was still a Panzer grenadier, but he didn't want to sit on top of a tank at the rear. He said, "Man, that is too dangerous for me, I am an only son. Let me go to the rear." But he was ordered with his squad - about twenty of them - into the trenches in front of our tanks, and he was killed by a direct hit, together with the other two men in the hole. He died there. I had to identify him later.

"We were attacked from the air many times by the Russian planes. I was in a

tank of the company Commander - I was told later that we had broken through the enemy lines on such and such an occasion and that later we could read all about it in books - which I have actually - but mostly, in those days, we retreated.

"We hadn't had any losses until then. All ten of our company tanks were present, except that we had no more fuel. We positioned ourselves behind a hill - our company Commander was called Werner Scherp, he got the Knight's Cross for this action - within 20 minutes we had destroyed five T-34's with our own tank. Every shell a hit! We could fire quite accurately, that was our advantage. The Russians were numerically superior but our firing was accurate and they couldn't get us because we only had the turret visible behind the hill. We even had equipment for seeing at night. To keep it short, we used five of the ten tanks as towing vehicles and set off for West Brem. Eventually we had to blow up all ten tanks because we had no more fuel. A very expensive exercise, and very sad too."

TRANSPORT ISSUES

In operations such as Spring Awakening, entire Panzer Divisions had to be moved all the way across Europe. The cumbersome process of loading and transporting an entire Panzer Division for transport from west to east was an enormously complex operation, but it was one which had been carried out a number of times. The standard procedure for moving a Panzer Division by rail had not escaped the all-seeing eyes of Allied intelligence, and was published in the US Army Handbook of 1945;

"STANDARD TROOP TRAINS. The Germans have found it desirable to use troop trains of a reasonably constant composition. The standard trains found in the Balkans, Italy, and Norway are composed of fewer cars than the base types in Germany, Denmark, and the Netherlands which are described below. All types are designed as far as possible to carry a self-contained unit such as a company or a battalion. Non-standard trains also may be used for troop movements.

"K-trains (Kraftfahrzüge or motor vehicle trains) average 51 cars per train and carry approximately 250 soldiers, 20 heavy vehicles (weighing up to 22 short tons per vehicle), and 20 light vehicles, plus other equipment. If lighter equipment is carried, the number of soldiers can be increased.

"S-trains (Sonderzüge, or special trains) are made up for the movement of

Captured Russian T-34 tanks are sent into action with German markings, manned by SS crews.

very heavy tanks and self-propelled guns. The number of men carried per train averages 125; the number of cars forming the train is between 30 and 35. An S-train usually carries from four to six Tiger tanks or from six to eight Panther tanks, interspersed with lighter equipment.

"Sp-trains (Sonderpanzerzüge, or special tank trains) carry approximately 20 medium tanks together with personnel and other equipment. The standard Sp-train is composed of about 33 cars.

"I-trains (Infanteriezüge or infantry trains) of about 55 cars per train hold some 350 officers and men, 10 light vehicles, 10 heavy vehicles of a maximum weight of 22 short tons per vehicle, and 70 horses, together with other equipment. If a minimum of equipment is carried, up to 800 troops can be moved. It is possible that the I-trains seldom are used by the Germans at present."

SOVIET CAPTURED TANKS

In 1943 a new generation of heavy tanks entered production - the Josef Stalin series. The JS-1 was a development of the KV series of heavy tanks with numerous improvements and modifications. The JS-1 was an interim model on the move

A Panzer IV being transported to the front on railway carriages. Judging by the excellent state of repair it looks as if this machine has proabaly come straight from the factory.

towards the JS-2 and only 102 were produced in 1943. These early tanks were armed with the same 85mm gun as the T-34/85. Later they were equipped with a 100mm main gun. In 1944 all existing JS-ls were re-armed with 122mm guns and were followed by the JS-2, which was an improved version and was to be the main production model. From 1943 to the end of the war 3,854 JS-2 tanks, including rebuilt JS-1 tanks, were produced. There is no evidence of JS tanks ever being used by the Germans, but knocked out examples were carefully examined and probably a single JS was provided to German Army Office for examination and testing purposes. The JS-2 was designated by the Germans as Panzerkampfwagen JS-122(r).

As the war progressed the Soviet Army began receiving the SU (Samokhadnaja Ustanovka) and JSU series. The SU-76 and SU-122 both appeared in 1942 in very limited numbers, eventually being followed by SU-85 and the SU-152 in 1943 and the SL-100 in 1944. Both the JSU-122 and the JSU-152 also appeared in 1943 in limited numbers.

The SU-76 and SU-76M assault guns were based on lengthened T-70 light tank chassis mounted with the superstructure open at the top and rear housing a 76.2mm gun. It was operated by a four-man crew and only 26 were produced in 1942, but eventually 12,671 were built by the end of the war. It is known that the Germans captured and pressed a number of SU-76 into service, and they were relatively easy to maintain, because the Panzerwaffe already used T-70 light tanks, and 76.2mm ammunition was widely available. In addition to the SU-76s used by Germans on the Eastern front at least one saw service during the Ardennes Offensive in December of 1944 with a Waffen-SS unit. Before the Ardennes offensive, this particular assault gun was in service on the Eastern Front and was transferred along with its unit to the Western Front. The SU-76 was either designated as Panzerjäger SU76(r) or Sturmgeschütz SU-76(r).

The SU-122 assault howitzer was based on a T-34 with its turret replaced by a fully enclosed armoured superstructure housing a 122mm howitzer. It was operated by a five-man crew and only 25 were produced in 1942, but eventually 1,148 were produced by 1944, when production switched to SU085. The Panzerwaffe captured and pressed a number into service. The Germans encountered few problems maintaining the SU-122 because it was based on the T-34 medium tank and 122mm ammunition was also widely available. It was designated by the Germans as Sturmgeschütz SU-122(r) / Stug.122(r). A single SU-22 was captured by Schwere Panzer Abteilung 502 on the Leningrad front in November 1943 and was also pressed into service.

The SU-85 tank destroyer was basically a modified SU-122 mounted with an 85mm gun and operated by a four-man crew. 2,050 were produced in 1944. In 1945 the SU-85 was replaced by the SU-100 tank destroyer. The SU-100 was an improved version of SU-85 armed with the 100mm gun. 1,675 SU-100 tank destroyers were produced from 1944 to the end of the war. The SU-85 was designated by the Germans as Jagdpanzer SU-85(r) and SU-100 as Jagdpanzer SU-100(r). It is known that the Russian volunteer units (possibly Kaminski Brigade) serving with the German Army used a small number of captured SU-85 tank destroyers.

The SU-152 was based on the KV-1 heavy tank mounted with a fully enclosed armoured superstructure housing a 152mm howitzer. Only 704 were produced in 1943, but the SU-152 proved to be successful when dealing with German Panther and Tiger tanks and it was nicknamed 'the animal killer'. The Germans captured a small number but there is no evidence of them being ever used, although a single example was captured by the Germans on 19th August 1943, following the Battle of Kursk Salient, and was probably handed over to the German Army Office for examination and tests. The captured SU-152 were designated as Sturmpanzer SU-152(r) or Sturmgeschütz SU-152(r).

The ISU-122 and ISU-I52 were further developments of the SU series but based on the chassis of the IS heavy tank series. The ISU-152 was armed with a 152mm howitzer and the ISU-122 was armed with a 122mm gun mounted in fully enclosed armoured superstructure. 4,075 were produced from 1943 to the end of the war. None was pressed into service and possibly a few captured examples were handed over to the German Army Office for examination and tests. ISU-122 was designated as Jagdpanzer JSU-122(r) and ISU-152 as Sturmpanzer JSU-152(r).

THE BATTLE FOR BERLIN

In February 1945 the last battle of the Second World War was drawing to a terrifying conclusion.

This, the most titanic of all conflicts, was certainly not about to end with a whimper. Although all hope of victory was long gone, the bitter fighting in the battle for Berlin would witness the frantic death throes of a desperate regime.

This was Hitler's long promised 'Gotterdämmerung' - the Twilight of the Gods. Those Gods would witness the agony of a city sacrificed to make a dramatic exit for one man.

Herr Ollech was one soldier who vividly recalled the collapsing German morale after the death of the Führer:

"We slept beside one another, we ate together, we were out there together in this misery, together we learned that Hitler had shot himself, that our 'all powerful father' was gone, we felt that we had been left behind, absolutely abandoned, he had deserted us, and what now..."

The tides of war were running inexorably against Germany. Hitler's thousand year Reich was already on its knees and it seemed there was a very real prospect of an end to the conflict before the end of the year.

From the skies over Germany, the Third Reich was experiencing destruction on a scale never before experienced by any nation at war. Hundreds of thousands of German civilians had perished in a series of raids which devastated German cities, among them the old port of Hamburg. In the wake of a heavy Allied bombing raid, Hamburg was swept by such intense firestorms that tornadoes were formed which sucked living people into the flames.

On land, too, the noose around Germany was tightening. In the west the Allies had at last established the long awaited second front, but it was in the east, in the cauldron of the Russian Front, that the events of the Second World War would be decided.

By October 1944 the German Army Group North besieging Leningrad had

The chassis of the 38(t) was also used to produce the Hetzer, an excellent tank-hunter design which packed a good punch fomr its 75mm gun, but produced a small silhouette which made it a difficult target to hit.

been driven back and was now trapped in the Kurland Bridgehead.

Following the success of Operation Bagration, the great offensive against Army Group Centre, Russian Armies were already on the border of Poland.

In the southern sector an unremitting pattern of defeat and retreat had seen the German forces driven back from Kharkov to the Balkans.

Faced with disaster on this scale the logical scenario would have been a German capitulation. In fact, the surviving German Armies continued to offer dogged resistance to the very last days of the war.

The effect of the military defeats of 1944 on Hitler was catastrophic. He began to hide himself away in his headquarters, embarrassed to face up to the hollowness of his earlier boasts. He found the psychological blows too great to rationalise. He was now unwilling to be seen in the newsreel footage, where once he had held centre stage. Those newsreels from the end of the war produce a picture of a broken, prematurely aged man. All traces of the confident leader have disappeared and his uncertain demeanour and hunched shoulders tell more of a story than words can. This was the man who was supposed to lead Germany through her greatest trial.

Happy Russian infantrymen inspect the results of their anti-tank expertise during the closing battles in the East.

Ranged against the crumbling German Armies was the immense strength of the Red Army and the revitalised Russian Air Force.

By now the German Army was massively outnumbered and the best estimates are that they possessed one tank for every 16 which the Russians could put into battle. It has been estimated that against the one million men Hitler could deploy, some five million Russians could be deployed for the battle of Berlin.

While the Western Allies concentrated on the strategic bombing campaign against German cities, the huge Russian bomber force was deployed against military targets on the ground. By late 1944 wave after wave of fighter-bombers flying overhead made it very difficult for German forces to move on the ground. The Russian Air Force was used as a prelude to all of the major offensives on the ground and it played a major part in achieving those victories.

The final assault on Germany itself began at the southern end of the front on 12th January 1945, when the massed tanks and infantry of the first Ukranian front under Marshal Koniev moved against the German lines. The advance of this front swept through Poland and saw the Russian Armies on the border with Czechoslovakia by the end of March.

To their north, the first Belorussian front under Zukhov swept aside the newly formed German Army Group A and, by the end of March, Zukhov's troops were positioned at Kustrin, only 50 miles from Hitler's capital.

Further north still, the last remnants of Army Group Centre were trapped in a huge pocket around Konigsberg; by the combined forces of the second and third Belorussioan fronts advancing from the north of Warsaw and Lithuania.

The rag-bag of forces fighting under SS Commander Himmler known as Army Group Vistula were also thrown back by the advancing Red Army.

The enormous sacrifice made by men fighting in what were obviously lost causes was justified by both the men and their commanders on the grounds that the continued resistance against the Soviet thrusts had allowed thousands of refugees to escape from the terror of the Red Army advance.

As they advanced into Germany, the Red Army had the opportunity to demonstrate that the forces of barbarism could be replaced by humanity. They chose instead to behave in a manner which aped the vile excesses of the regime against which they fought. With the blessing and participation of their officers, the men of the Soviet forces in Germany embarked on an unrestrained orgy of looting, murder and mass rape which, given all that had occurred in Russia, was to an extent predictable.

"The civilians were in the cellars, scared to death, old people, women and children. They only left the cellars to fetch water and maintain a minimum of hygiene: it was like that in the rest of Germany and also in Berlin. Scarcely anything to eat and in constant fear. Sadly, the Red Army made the mistake of turning fear into reality and raped the German women: sadly, those things happened which are incomprehensible now as they were then; if one really intends to forge a new future, then I don't quite understand it."

In the face of Red Army retribution the will to resist remained and in many cases German resistance actually began to increase: there were even successful counter-attacks which revealed to the Germans the level of the horrors that awaited them. Footage taken at a German town recaptured from the Russians shows evidence of atrocities committed while the town was briefly in Russian hands.

All that remained for the ordinary German citizen was to wait for the Red Army to regroup and gather its huge strength for the final assault on Berlin.

The grim joke began to do the rounds of war torn streets of Berlin – "Enjoy the war while you can because the peace will be terrible."

Faced with a doomsday scenario, organised German resistance continued and the final Soviet drive for Berlin could not begin in earnest until 16th April 1945.

Even if they had wanted to, Berliners simply could not hoist the while flag and surrender. Despite his pathetic condition, Hitler was still in control of Berlin, the SS and the Gestapo still functioned and he still gave the orders for the defence. And what Hitler demanded he got. Berlin was ultimately a battle which was fought virtually to the last bullet and almost to the last gasp. The German forces, which were still in the field, were determined to fight to the very end, so the closing battles of the war were as hotly contested as anything which had gone before. 55 years on from the events of the battle Herr Ollech recalled the fighting on the outskirts of Berlin:

"We were sent into action in the north-east of Berlin, and suddenly, as a young man - and you can see photos of me - I had to shoot at human beings in order to preserve my own life. You do not consciously experience that process, you only experience it in retrospect. Death does not only strike your comrade's, it strikes the enemy too. And for that reason I can only say that war is like diarrhoea. It is truly the lowest rung of humanity. And when your comrades fall beside you, and you are 17 years old, and are directly confronted, directly confronted with the events of war, it causes a change in your mentality."

Although they faced a number of insurmountable difficulties in supply and material the German forces fighting to defend Berlin prepared to do their duty with great courage and thoroughness. The east side of Berlin was strongly fortified with three separate lines of anti-tank defences. In the city itself every street was to be made a strong point. Hitler had hoped to turn Berlin into a fortress. Ringed around the city were three structures which harked back to the medieval castles of old. These were the flak towers, three huge concrete castles with walls so thick that not even the heaviest artillery shells could penetrate. The first was located just off the Brunnen Strasse in the north of the city and was known as the Humboldthain Tower. The second was just to the

A Panther is dug into the streets of Berlin to provide a fixed defensive position.

One of the best all-round fighting vehicles of the war was the Jagdpather. WIth well-shaped armour and the excellent 88mm main armament this machine was much feared by Allied tank crews.

east of the city centre on Landsberger Allee and the third was in the southwest of the city centre at the Berlin Zoo. Built in 1945, their real purpose was to serve as anti-aircraft gun platforms to protect the city against the frequent Allied bombing raids. Each of the enormous gun towers had a satellite tower a short distance away for the artillery observers to control the anti-aircraft fire. Now, with the Soviet forces beginning to encroach on Berlin itself, they were to become a vital part of the defence ring hastily thrown up around the city. These defences were designed to protect the heart of the Nazi regime located in a bunker close to the Chancellery building in Wilhelm Strasse. Nearby were the city landmarks of the Brandenburg Gate on the Unter Den Linden and the Reichstag on Königsplatz. All of these sites were to see savage fighting in the coming battle, and the makeshift defences would take an enormous toll from the Soviet forces – 333,000 casualties before they finally clawed their way into the Reichstag.

There were still substantial Wehrmacht elements who fought to the bitter end, but they were now augmented by the men of the Volkssturm battalions; these were scratch formations composed of old men and young boys who were now literally fighting to defend their own homes and families; this was to prove a forlorn hope.

Before they were swept aside, the men of the Volkssturm had become highly proficient in the use of the Panzerfaust, which was an anti-tank weapon of deadly effectiveness at short range.

One additional obstacle which the Russians would have to overcome were the wrecks of their own tanks, which frequently formed a convenient barricade across many of the streets, where they had come to grief against these hand held rockets which made the humble infantryman the equal of the mighty T-34.

The German tank formations had been largely destroyed but in the rubble-strewn streets of German towns and cities tankhunting teams could get to close quarters, and the Panzerfausts claimed hundreds of Russian tanks destroyed at close range by desperate men fighting in their own city. But there were other occasions where the Volkssturm proved less than resolute, as Hen Ollech recalled:

"We spent that night there and the next morning, the weather was dry. We discovered that the infantry units, in the shape of the Volkssturm which was supposed to be in front of us and whom we had seen the day before, had vanished. That, of course, scared the wits out of us and then we got the order to retreat with our unit into the town proper, because the Red Army, primarily the infantry, but also the tanks, had already gone around us and broken through into the suburbs. If we hadn't changed positions, they would have had us encircled."

Hitler had by now become mesmerised by the arrows on the situation map in the bunker; reduced to clutching at straws, he began to believe once again that the flags on the map represented real military forces. In particular Hitler began to believe that Steiner's 11th Army could somehow link-up with the surviving German forces north of Berlin and strike a decisive blow against the Russians. In reality the grand sounding title of Army was illusory. The ragbag of forces at Steiner's disposal could only be described as an Army in the deranged mind of Adolf Hitler; in fact, the depleted forces available to the German commanders still fighting on the outskirts of the city had no real prospect of halting the Soviet advance, never mind any question of reversing the tide.

The battered German defenders had managed to mount a spirited defence on the Seelow heights to the east of Berlin, but the Soviet juggernaut in the form of devastating massed artillery attacks made the position untenable.

With the last natural obstacle against a Russian advance neutralised the Soviets could now advance on the city itself.

"The news came that the Soviets were advancing along this road which only became understandable in retrospect; they could see with the naked eye whether or not mines had been laid.

It was an asphalt road so they could see exactly that it had not been laid with mines; as the road was free of mines they advanced. Along it came four T-34's, two Shermans and an assault tank. The road had a small bend and, before the first tank had reached this bend, it was fired at and everything blew apart. We had an artillery gun, the 88mm which had a velocity of 1,200 metres per second, the only gun in the world from which the shell left the barrel at such speed. That meant that the discharge and impact, especially at a distance of 200, perhaps 300, metres, was so short, that you thought that discharge and impact was the same sound. These tanks were soon all destroyed and the Red Army infantry that sat on the rear of the tanks had already dispersed. The tanks glowed throughout that night and if there was ammunition inside it exploded. We spent the night there; we felt like big game hunters. You know, a hunter is happy when he has killed the game."

Despite the best efforts of hard-pressed men like Herr Ollech, the noose was tightening. Against this gloomy scenario. Hitler hung on to the hope of relief by General Hienrici with the 9th Army, but Hienrici was no fool and he knew a lost cause when he saw one. In order to prevent needless bloodshed in a final pointless gesture Hienrici moved his Army away from the beleaguered city leaving Hitler to fume in his lair.

Matters took a further turn for the worse when Steiner's 11th Army was brushed aside to allow the Russians to complete the encirclement of Berlin. By 22nd April Russian troops were fighting on the streets of the German capital; both sides knew the insanity was surely about to end. But in the unconquered portions of the city the street warfare in Berlin raged on as bitterly as ever.

Any prospect of a wholesale evacuation for the Führer and his entourage had now disappeared and a radio broadcast on 22nd April announced that the

Even in the closing months of the war work continued on tank development programms. Despite the lessons of the Tiger II, research was still carried out into the super heavy Maus.

Führer would stay in his capital to the very last.

The cumulative effect of years of Allied bombing and the devastation caused by the heavy Russian artillery barrage had created a wilderness of rubble full of ready-made strong points, which naturally favoured the defender. Throughout the city fierce street fighting continued to rage unabated, as the Red Army fought bitterly all the way to the Reichstag.

The final Russian assault on Berlin began on 26th April; it was preceded by very heavy air attacks and, as always, a thunderous artillery barrage. It was now that the battles for the flak towers began.

Among the last defenders was Herr Ollech, who had retreated with the survivors of his unit to the Humboldthain flak tower, which housed 30,000 terrified civilians in addition to the military garrison.

"We retreated and retreated, and we finally ended up in a flak tower. There were three of them in Berlin, and we got ourselves over to one of them. Our commander was a Colonel Schafer - and the Soviet Army fired at the tower with their tanks. You could hear the tanks firing at the tower, and it went 'clack-clack' as if someone was knocking on a door: The Red Army discovered that they were not going to get anywhere like that: shooting at it with a 76mm wouldn't achieve anything. So, over a period of days, they brought up 15cm howitzers and they could fire directly at the tower; so they let loose with direct fire from the 15cm. That still only managed to make tiny holes in the concrete. There were windows which were closed from the outside with heavy steel doors. I imagine that they weighed tons, and the Russians at last succeeded in hitting the upper hinge of one of the doors which burst and one of these broke off, twisted off the other and hurtled downwards; and that was the only hole that existed. They then brought up a light artillery piece. A tank attack at night followed; they knew that we were lying in relays in the surrounding trenches. We had never experienced that before, tanks at night, and that was the most serious, perhaps the most awful experience, because they attacked and we sought cover, had to lay down on our fallen comrades. We fought off the attack, and the next morning we were able to see the burnt out tanks and the Russian corpses hanging over the edges of their trenches, their machine guns dragged halfway in. They were on wheels which you could hear when they were crossing a street because they rattled 'rat-a-tat' over the street, they

One of the most bizarre ideas to emerge from the drawing boards of German tank designers was this curious machine, known variously as the Grille, Cricket or Grasshopper. The idea was that the machine would use its tracks to move into action then detach the turrent to form a mobile pillbox.

dragged it behind them; that was fought off."

While Herr Ollech and his colleagues were fighting their desperate battles, Hitler remained in his bunker. On the night of 28th April, with the Russian forces grinding ever closer to his headquarters, he married his mistress, Eva Braun. After the wedding meal he retired to write his last will and testament. He defiantly reaffirmed his belief in Liebensraum and indulged in one last vitriolic attack on the Jewish race. On the afternoon of 30th April, having made his farewells, he poisoned his wife and his dog and shot himself.

On the same evening that Hitler committed suicide, the last battle was raging for the Reichstag. The indomitable defenders had bricked up the windows and doors and now made a desperate last stand which had to be overcome room by room. With the Germans inside still resisting, Sergeants Yagorov and Kantariya planted the Victory Banner of the Soviet flag on the Reichstag at 10.50pm. It symbolised the triumph of the Soviet Union over Nazi Germany but it still remained a symbolic act.

Despite all of the enormous difficulties under which they now laboured, the logistical services of the German Armed Forces continued to produce minor miracles of supply, which allowed some fairly formidable tank formations to enter the final battle for Berlin. Among them was the 503rd heavy tank battalion equipped with the mighty King Tiger tank.

These impressive machines fought alongside the 11th SS Division 'Nordland' and, even more remarkably, a battalion of French volunteers which had formed a part of the 'Charlemagne' Division. On 25th April there were still 300 men available for combat in the French volunteer battalion. Together these two formations played a key role in the defence of the government buildings in the centre of Berlin. In many respects the Frenchmen had nothing to lose and there was even less at stake for their German masters.

The SS, in particular, knew that they could expect no mercy from the Red Army which had long since adopted the practice of shooting SS prisoners out of hand. Perhaps it was this knowledge which kept many formations at their post during the dark days of the battles for Berlin, but as late as 26th April the commander of the 503rd heavy tank battalion was able to report that he still had six tanks ready for active service in the defence of the routes leading to the centre of Berlin. Even more remarkably, they also had stocks of fuel

Despite the rapidly deteriorating situation, the German tank designers continued to develop the next generation of tanks including the master, this E-series prototype for a super-heavy tank to rival the Maus.

and a plentiful supply of ammunition, including the bulky 88mm ammunition for the massive high-velocity guns which were carried in the turrets of these formidable machines.

Backed up by the Panzerfausts of the French and Norwegian volunteers, this small battle group claimed dozens of Russian tanks during the bitter street fighting which marked the very last days of the Third Reich.

Incredibly, even the back-up and repair services of the remaining German tank battalions continued to function and, by 1st May, five days after Hitler's death, the number of tanks available to the 503rd heavy tank battalion had actually increased, and there were now 11 tanks ready for action in the bitter street battles which continued as the diehards fought to maintain their shrinking perimeter.

In his memoirs, Marshal Koniev admitted that the Soviet Army had lost 800 tanks in the fighting for Berlin. In many respects this last nut was the toughest that the Red Army had to crack.

The Russians had announced that they would capture Berlin on 1st May but the beleaguered defenders took perverse pride in the fact that by the morning of 2nd May there was still fierce resistance in some sectors of the city. Although the official surrender took place on the afternoon of 2nd May, a number of German units nonetheless attempted to break out of the Soviet sector and make their way towards the Western Allies with the result that Berlin was not finally pacified until 3rd May.

After the surrender, the city authorities estimated that there had been something like 90,000 instances of rape in the last few days before the surrender of the city. For the ordinary citizens of Berlin there could be no prospect of relief.

Although military discipline would soon be restored, it was obvious that one barbarous and inhuman regime had been swapped for another. As East Germans, three generations of Berliners would pay a heavy price for loyalty to the man who did not possess the personal courage to face the music.

APPENDIX

DIVISIONS

DIVISIONS	RECRUITING DISTRICT	DIVISIONAL ELEMENTS	COMBAT HISTORY
1st Panzer	IX (Kassel) Formed Oct. 1935	1st Panzer Regt 1st Panzer Grenadier Regt 113th Panzer Grenadier Regt 75th Panzer Artillery Regt 1st Artillery Panzer Section	Poland 1939 Belgium 1940 France 1940 Russia 1941-43 (Leningrad, Moscow) Balkans 1943 Russia 1944 (Zhitomir, Cherkassy Relief, Hubes Pocket) Hungary & Austria 1945
2nd Panzer	XVII (Vienna) Formed Oct. 1935	3rd Panzer Regt 2nd Panzer Grenadier Regt 304th Panzer Grenadier Regt 74th Panzer Artillery Regt 2nd Reconnaissance Section	Poland 1939 France 1940 Balkans 1941 Russia 1942-43 (Rshev, Kursk, Kiev) France 1944 (Falaise, Ardennes) Germany 1945
3rd Panzer	III (Berlin) Formed Oct. 1935	6th Panzer Regt 3rd Panzer Grenadier Regt 394th Panzer Grenadier Regt 75th Panzer Artillery Regt 3rd Reconnaissance Section	Poland 1939 France 1940 Russia 1941-43 (Smolensk, Kiev, Tula, Kursk, Kharkov, Cherkassy Relief) Poland 1944 Hungary & Austria 1945
4th Panzer	XIII (Nuremberg) Formed Nov. 1938	35th Panzer Regt 12th Panzer Grenadier Regt 38th Panzer Grenadier Regt 103rd Panzer Artillery Regt 4th Reconnaissance Section	Poland 1939 France 1940 Russia 1941-44 (Caucasus, Kursk, Latvia) Germany 1945

DIVISIONS	RECRUITING DISTRICT	DIVISIONAL ELEMENTS	COMBAT HISTORY
5th Panzer	VIII (Breslau) Formed Nov. 1938	31st Panzer Regt 13th Panzer Grenadier Regt 14th Panzer Grenadier Regt 116th Panzer Artillery Regt 5th Reconnaissance Section	France 1940 Balkans 1941 Russia 1941-44 (Kursk, Dnieper, Latvia) East Prussia 1944-45
6th Panzer	VI (Munster) Formed Oct. 1939	11th Panzer Regt 4th Panzer Grenadier Regt 114th Panzer Grenadier Regt 76th Panzer Artillery Regt 6th Reconnaissance Section	Russia 1941-44 France 1944 Hungary & Austria 1944-45
7th Panzer	IX (Kassel) Formed Oct. 1939	25th Panzer Regt 6th Panzer Grenadier Regt 7th Panzer Grenadier Regt 78th Panzer Artillery Regt 7th Reconnaissance Section	France 1940 Russia 1941-42 (Kalinin, Rshev) Southern Russia 1942-44 (Kharkov, Kursk, Kiev, Zhitomir, Hubes Pocker) Baltic Coast & Prussia 1944-45
8th Panzer	III (Berlin) Formed Oct. 1939	10th Panzer Regt 8th Panzer Grenadier Regt 28th Panzer Grenadier Regt 80th Panzer Artillery Regt 8th Reconnaissance Section	France 1940 Yugoslavia 1941 Northern Russia 1941-43 (Leningrad, Kholm, Orel, Kiev) Southern Russia 1943-44 Hungary & Yugoslavia 1944-45
9th Panzer	XVII (Vienna) Formed Aug. 1940	33rd Panzer Regt 10th Panzer Grenadier Regt 11th Panzer Grenadier Regt 102nd Panzer Artillery Regt 9th Reconnaissance Section	Netherlands & France 1940 Balkans 1941 Russia 1941-44

DIVISIONS	RECRUITING DISTRICT	DIVISIONAL ELEMENTS	COMBAT HISTORY
10th Panzer	V (Stuttgart) Formed April 1939	7th Panzer Regt 69th Panzer Grenadier Regt 86th Panzer Grenadier Regt 90th Panzer Artillery Regt 10th Reconnaissance Section	Poland 1939 France 1940 Russia 1941-42 Tunisia 1943 (Kasserine, Medenine, Tunisia)
11th Panzer	VIII (Breslau) Formed Aug. 1940	15th Panzer Regt 110th Panzer Grenadier Regt 111th Panzer Grenadier Regt 119th Panzer Artillery Regt 11th Reconnaissance Section	Balkans 1941 Russia 1941-44 (Moscow, Kharkov, Kursk, Cherkasssy, Hubes Pocket) North West Europe 1944-45 (Ardennes, Remagen)
12th Panzer	II (Stettin) Formed Oct. 1940	29th Panzer Regt 5th Panzer Grenadier Regt 25th Panzer Grenadier Regt 2nd Panzer Artillery Regt 12th Reconnaissance Section	Russia 1941-44 (Smolensk, Leningrad, Orel & Middle Dnepr)
13th Panzer	XI (Hannover) Formed Oct. 1940	4th Panzer Regt 66th Panzer Grenadier Regt 93rd Panzer Grenadier Regt 13th Panzer Artillery Regt 13th Reconnaissance Section	Russia 1941-44 (Kiev, Caucasus, Kuban) Romania 1944 Hungary 1944-45
14th Panzer	IV (Dresden) Formed Aug. 1940	36th Panzer Regt 103rd Panzer Grenadier Regt 108th Panzer Regt 4th Panzer Artillery Regt 14th Reconnaissance Section	Yugoslavia 1941 Southern Russia 1941-42 Russia 1943-45 (Dnepr Bend, Ukraine, Kurland)

DIVISIONS	RECRUITING DISTRICT	DIVISIONAL ELEMENTS	COMBAT HISTORY
15th Panzer	(Darmstadt / Landau) Deutsches Afrika Korps Formed Aug. 1940	8th Panzer Regt 104th Panzer Grenadier Regt 115th Panzer Grenadier Regt 33rd Panzer Artillery Regt 15th Reconnaissance Section	North Africa 1941
16th Panzer	VI (Munster) Formed Aug. 1940	2nd Panzer Regt 64th Panzer Grenadier Regt 79th Panzer Grenadier Regt 16th Panzer Artillery Regt 16th Reconnaissance Section	Souhern Russia 1941-42 Italy 1943 (Salerno, Naples) Russia 1943-45
17th Panzer	VII (Munich) Formed Oct. 1940	39th Panzer Regt 40th Panzer Grenadier Regt 63rd Panzer Grenadier Regt 27th Panzer Artillery Regt 17th Reconnaissance Section	Russia 1941-45 (Smolensk, Kiev, Stalingrad (relief), Kharkov, Cherkassy, Hubes Pocket)
18th Panzer	IV (Dresden) Formed Oct. 1940	18th Panzer Regt 52nd Panzer Grenadier Regt 101st Panzer Grenadier Regt 88th Panzer Artillery Regt 8th Reconnaissance Section	Russia 1941-43 Lithuania 1944
19th Panzer	XI (Hannover) Formed Oct. 1940	27th Panzer Regt 73rd Panzer Grenadier Regt 74th Panzer Grenadier Regt 19th Panzer Artillery Regt 19th Reconnaissance Section	Russia 1941-44 (Minsk, Smolensk, Veliki Luki, Moscow, Kharkov, Kursk) East Prussia 1944
20th Panzer	XI (Hannover) Formed Oct. 1940	21st Panzer Regt 59th Panzer Grenadier Regt 112th Panzer Grenadier Regt 92nd Panzer Artillery Regt 20th Reconnaissance Section	Russia 1941-44 (Moscow, Kursk) Romania 1944 East Prussia 1944 Hungary 1944

DIVISIONS	RECRUITING DISTRICT	DIVISIONAL ELEMENTS	COMBAT HISTORY
21st Panzer	Formed Feb. 1941 in North Africa (From 5th Light Afrikan District)	22nd Panzer Regt 125th Panzer Grenadier Regt 192nd Panzer Grenadier Regt 155th Panzer Artillery Regt 21st Reconnaissance Section	North Africa 1941 France 1943-44 Germany 1945
22nd Panzer	XII (Wiesbaden) Formed Oct. 1941	204th Panzer Regt 129th Panzer Grenadier Regt 140th Panzer Grenadier Regt 140th Panzer Artillery Regt 140th Reconnaissance Section	Russian Front 1942 (Stalingrad)
23rd Panzer	XII (Stuttgart) Formed Oct. 1941 in France from around Paris	23rd Panzer Regt 126th Panzer Grenadier Regt 128th Panzer Grenadier Regt 128th Panzer Artillery Regt 23rd Reconnaissance Section	Russia 1942-44 (Kharkov, Caucasus, Stalingrad, Dnepr Bend) Poland & Hungary 1944
24th Panzer	I (Konigsberg) Formed Feb. 1942	24th Panzer Regt 21st Panzer Grenadier Regt 26th Panzer Grenadier Regt 89th Panzer Artillery Regt 24th Reconnaissance Section	Russia 1941 (Stalingrad) Poland 1944 Hungary 1944 East Prussia 1945
25th Panzer	VI (Munster) Formed Feb. 1942 from occupation units in Norway	9th Panzer Regt 146th Panzer Regt 147th Panzer Regt 91st Panzer Artillery Regt 25th Reconnaissance Section	France 1943 Southern Russia 1943 (Kiev) Warsaw 1944 Germany 1945
26th Panzer	III (Berlin) Formed Oct. 1942	26th Panzer Regt 9th Panzer Grenadier Regt 67th Panzer Grenadier Regt 93rd Panzer Artillery Regt 26th Reconnaissance Section	Italy 1943 (Anzio, Cassino) Adriatic Coast 1944

DIVISIONS	RECRUITING DISTRICT	DIVISIONAL ELEMENTS	COMBAT HISTORY
27th Panzer	Formed 1942	140th Panzer Grenadier Regt 127th Panzer Artillery Regt	Russia 1942
116th Panzer	VI (Munster) Formed April 1944 in France	16th Panzer Regt 60th Panzer Grenadier Regt 156th Panzer Grenadier Regt 146th Panzer Artillery Regt 116th Reconnaissance Section	Ardennes 1944-45
Panzer-Lehr	Formed in France in 1944	103rd Panzer Lehr Regt 901st Panzer Grenadier Regt 902nd Panzer Grenadier Regt 130th Panzer Artillery Lehr Regt 130th Reconnaissance Lehr Regt	France 1944 Hungary 1944 Germany 1944
1st Feld-Herrnhalle Panzer (FHH1)	Formed Sept. 1944 in Hungary	Had no established divisional strength.	Budapest 1945
3rd Panzer Grenadier	Based on III (Berlin) Formed Oct. 1934	8th Panzer Grenadier Regt 28th Panzer Grenadier Regt 103rd Panzer Batallion 3rd Artillery Regt 103rd Reconnaissance Section	Eastern Front 1941 Stalingrad 1943
10th Panzer Grenadier	Based on XIII (Nuremberg) Formed Oct. 1934	20th Panzer Grenadier Regt 41st Panzer Grenadier Regt 7th Panzer Batallion 10th Artillery Regt 110th Reconnaissance Section	Eastern Front 1941 Demjansk 1943 Radom 1945
14th Motorised Infantry Division	Formed Oct. 1934	11th Panzer Grenadier Regt 53rd Panzer Grenadier Regt 114th Reconnaissance Section	Eastern Front 1941 Rshev 1943

DIVISIONS	RECRUITING DISTRICT	DIVISIONAL ELEMENTS	COMBAT HISTORY
16th Panzer Grenadier	Based on VI (Munster) Formed Aug. 1940	60th Panzer Grenadier Regt 156th Panzer Grenadier Regt 116th Panzer Batallion 146th Artillery Regt 116th Reconnaissance Section	Yugoslavia 1941 Don. Rostov 1943
18th Panzer Grenadier	Based on VIII (Breslau) Formed Oct. 1934	30th Panzer Grenadier Regt 51st Panzer Grenadier Regt 118th Panzer Batallion 118th Artillery Regt 118th Reconnaissance Section	Poland 1939 France 1940 Eastern Front 1941 Staraya 1943
20th Panzer Grenadier	Based on V (Hamburg) Formed Oct. 1934	76th Panzer Grenadier Regt 90th Panzer Grenadier Regt 8th Panzer Batallion 20th Artillery Regt 120th Reconnaissance Section	Poland 1939 France 1940 Eastern Front 1941 (Minsk, Bialystok)
25th Panzer Grenadier	Based on V (Stuttgart) Formed April 1936	35th Panzer Grenadier Regt 119th Panzer Grenadier Regt 5th Panzer Batallion 25th Artillery Regt 126th Reconnaissance Section	France 1940 Germany 1940 Eastern Front 1941 (Zhitomir, Uman, Kiev)
29th Panzer Grenadier	Based on IX (Kassel) Formed Oct. 1936	15th Panzer Grenadier Regt 71st Panzer Grenadier Regt 129th Panzer Batallion 129th Artillery Regt 129th Reconnaissance Section	Poland 1939 France 1940 Germany 1941 Eastern Front 1941 (Minsk, Smolensk, Bryansk)
36th Motorised Infantry	Formed Oct. 1936	87th Panzer Grenadier Regt 118th Panzer Grenadier Regt 136th Reconnaissance Section	Germany 1941 Eastern Front 1941 (Pleskau, Leningrad)
60th Motorised Infantry Division	Based on XX (Danzig) Formed Oct. 1939	92nd Motorised Grenadier Regt 120th Motorised Grenadier Regt 160th Panzer Batallion 160th Artillery Regt 160th Reconnaissance Section	Eastern Front 1941 Demjansk 1943 Radom 1945

SS PANZER & PANZER GRENADIER DIVISIONS	RECRUITING DISTRICT	DIVISIONAL ELEMENTS	COMBAT HISTORY
1st SS Panzer Grenadier "Liebstandarte Adolf Hitler"	Formed March 1933 from Hitler's bodyguard troops	1st SS Panzer Grenadier Regt 2nd SS Panzer Grenadier Regt 1st SS Panzer Regt 1st SS Panzer Artillery Regt	Poland 1939 Holland 1940 Balkans 1941 Italy 1943
2nd SS Panzer Grenadier "Das Reich"	Formed Oct. 1939	3rd SS Panzer Grenadier Regt 4th SS Panzer Grenadier Regt 2nd SS Panzer Regt 2nd SS Panzer Artillery Regt	Holland 1940 Balkans 1941 Russia 1943
3rd SS Panzer Grenadier	Totenkopf Formed Nov. 1939	5th SS Panzer Grenadier Regt 6th SS Panzer Grenadier Regt 3rd SS Panzer Regt 3rd SS Panzer Artillery Regt	France 1940 Germany 1941 Poland 1944
4th SS Panzer Grenadier "Polizei"	Formed Sept. 1939 (Disbanded in 1942)	7th SS Panzer Grenadier Regt 8th SS Panzer Grenadier Regt 4th SS Panzer Regt 4th SS Panzer Artillery Regt	Eastern Front 1941 (Dunaburg, Luga, Leningrad) Yugoslavia 1944
5th SS Panzer Grenadier "Wiking"	Formed Dec. 1940	9th SS Panzer Grenadier Regt 10th SS Panzer Grenadier Regt 5th SS Panzer Regt 5th SS Panzer Artillery Regt	Eastern Front 1941 (Tarnopol, Zhitomir, Azov, Rostov) Warsaw 1944
9th SS Panzer Grenadier "Hohenstaufen"	Formed March 1943 at Mailly-Le-Camp	19th SS Panzer Grenadier Regt 20th SS Panzer Grenadier Regt 9th SS Panzer Regt 9th SS Panzer Artillery Regt	Poland 1944

SS PANZER & PANZER GRENADIER DIVISIONS	RECRUITING DISTRICT	DIVISIONAL ELEMENTS	COMBAT HISTORY
10th SS Panzer Grenadier "Frundsberg"	Formed Feb. 1943	21st SS Panzer Grenadier Regt 22nd SS Panzer Grenadier Regt 10th SS Panzer Regt 10th SS Panzer Artillery Regt	Poland 1944
11th SS Freiwillige Panzer Grenadier "Nordland"	Formed Mat 1943	23rd SS Panzer Grenadier Regt 24th SS Panzer Grenadier Regt 11th SS Panzer Regt 11th SS Panzer Artillery Regt	Eastern Front 1943 (Leningrad)
12th SS Panzer Grenadier "Hitler Jugend"	Formed July 1943	SS Panzer Grenadier Regt SS Panzer Grenadier Regt SS Panzer Regt SS Panzer Artillery Regt	Ardennes 1944 Hungary 1945
16th SS Panzer Grenadier "Reichs Fuhrer"	Formed May 1941	SS Panzer Grenadier Regt SS Panzer Grenadier Regt SS Panzer Regt SS Panzer Artillery Regt	Corsica 1943 Italy 1944 Hungary 1945
17th SS Panzer Grenadier "Goetz von Berlichingen"	Formed Oct. 1943	SS Panzer Grenadier Regt SS Panzer Grenadier Regt SS Panzer Regt SS Panzer Artillery Regt	France 1944 Metz 1944 France 1945
18th SS Freiwillige Panzer Grenadier "Horst Wessel"	Formed Feb. 1944	SS Panzer Grenadier Regt SS Panzer Grenadier Regt SS Panzer Regt SS Panzer Artillery Regt	Hungary 1944
23rd SS Freiwillige Panzer Grenadier "Nederland"	Formed July 1943	SS Panzer Grenadier Regt SS Panzer Grenadier Regt SS Panzer Regt SS Panzer Artillery Regt	Hungary 1943
27th SS Freiwillige Panzer Grenadier "Langemarck"	Formed May 1943	SS Panzer Grenadier Regt SS Panzer Grenadier Regt SS Panzer Regt SS Panzer Artillery Regt	Poland 1943 Russia 1944 (Zhitomir)

SS PANZER & PANZER GRENADIER DIVISIONS	RECRUITING DISTRICT	DIVISIONAL ELEMENTS	COMBAT HISTORY
28th SS Freiwillige Panzer Grenadier "Wallonien"	Formed July 1943	SS Panzer Grenadier Regt SS Panzer Grenadier Regt SS Panzer Regt SS Panzer Artillery Regt	Russia 1943 (Dnieper) Germany 1944
38th SS Panzer Grenadier "Nibelungen"	Formed March 1945	Composition unknown	Germany 1945

A Tiger II of s.H.Pz.Abt. 503 and Hungarian troops in a battle scarred street in Buda's Castle district, October 1944

NUMBERING THE PANZER DIVISIONS

1939	1940	1941	1942	1943	1944	1945
1 Pz. Div.	1 Pz. Div.	1 Pz. Div.	1 Pz. Div.	1 Pz. Div.	1 Pz. Div.	1 Pz. Div.
2 Pz. Div.	2 Pz. Div.	2 Pz. Div.	2 Pz. Div.	2 Pz. Div.	2 Pz. Div.	2 Pz. Div.
3 Pz. Div.	3 Pz. Div.	3 Pz. Div.	3 Pz. Div.	3 Pz. Div.	3 Pz. Div.	3 Pz. Div.
4 Pz. Div.	4 Pz. Div.	4 Pz. Div.	4 Pz. Div.	4 Pz. Div.	4 Pz. Div.	4 Pz. Div.
5 Pz. Div.	5 Pz. Div.	5 Pz. Div.	5 Pz. Div.	5 Pz. Div.	5 Pz. Div.	5 Pz. Div.
1 Lt. Div.	Converted from Lt. to 6 Pz. Div.	6 Pz. Div.	6 Pz. Div.	6 Pz. Div.	6 Pz. Div.	6 Pz. Div.
2 Lt. Div.	Converted from Lt. to 7 Pz. Div.	7 Pz. Div.	7 Pz. Div.	7 Pz. Div.	7 Pz. Div.	7 Pz. Div.
3 Lt. Div.	Converted from Lt. to 8 Pz. Div.	8 Pz. Div.	8 Pz. Div.	8 Pz. Div.	8 Pz. Div.	8 Pz. Div.
4 Lt. Div.	Converted from Lt. to 9 Pz. Div.	9 Pz. Div.	9 Pz. Div.	9 Pz. Div.	9 Pz. Div.	9 Pz. Div.
10 Pz. Div.	10 Pz. Div.	10 Pz. Div.	10 Pz. Div.	10 Pz. Div.		
		11 Pz. Div.	11 Pz. Div.	11 Pz. Div.	11 Pz. Div.	11 Pz. Div.
			12 Pz. Div.	12 Pz. Div.	12 Pz. Div.	12 Pz. Div.
			13 Pz. Div.	13 Pz. Div.	13 Pz. Div.	13 Pz. Div.
		12 Pz. Div.	12 Pz. Div.	12 Pz. Div.	12 Pz. Div.	12 Pz. Div.
		13 Pz. Div.	13 Pz. Div.	13 Pz. Div.	13 Pz. Div.	13 Pz. Div.
		14 Pz. Div.	14 Pz. Div.	14 Pz. Div.	14 Pz. Div.	14 Pz. Div.
		15 Pz. Div.	Became the 15th Grenadier Divsion			
		16 Pz. Div.	16 Pz. Div.	16 Pz. Div.	16 Pz. Div.	16 Pz. Div.
		17 Pz. Div.	17 Pz. Div.	17 Pz. Div.	17 Pz. Div.	17 Pz. Div.
		18 Pz. Div.	18 Pz. Div.	18 Pz. Div.	Reorganised as an Artillery Division	
	5 Lt. Div.					
		19 Pz. Div.	19 Pz. Div.	19 Pz. Div.	19 Pz. Div.	19 Pz. Div.
		20 Pz. Div.	20 Pz. Div.	20 Pz. Div.	20 Pz. Div.	20 Pz. Div.
		21 Pz. Div.	21 Pz. Div.	21 Pz. Div.	21 Pz. Div.	21 Pz. Div.
			22 Pz. Div.			
			23 Pz. Div.	23 Pz. Div.	23 Pz. Div.	23 Pz. Div.
			24 Pz. Div.	24 Pz. Div.	24 Pz. Div.	24 Pz. Div.
				25 Pz. Div.	1 Pz. Div.	1 Pz. Div.
				26 Pz. Div.	26 Pz. Div.	26 Pz. Div.
				27 Pz. Div.	27 Pz. Div.	27 Pz. Div.
		90 Lt. Div.	90 Lt. Div.	Converted to Panzer Grenadier Division		
		164 Lt. Div.	164 Lt. Div.			
				H. Göring	H. Göring	H. Göring
					FF H1	FF H1
					Norwegan	Norwegan
Gross	Gross				116 Pz. Div.	116 Pz. Div.
Deutschland	Deutschland				Pz. Lehr	Pz. Lehr
Pz. Gren Division	Pz. Gren Division	Gross	Gross	Gross	Gross	Gross
		Deutschland	Deutschland	Deutschland	Deutschland	Deutschland
		Pz. Gren Division	Pz. Gren Division	Pz. Gren Division	Pz. Gren Division	Pz. Gren Division

More from the same series

Most books from the 'Hitler's War Machine' series are edited and endorsed by Emmy Award winning film maker and military historian Bob Carruthers, producer of Discovery Channel's Line of Fire and Weapons of War and BBC's Both Sides of the Line. Long experience and strong editorial control gives the military history enthusiast the ability to buy with confidence.

Tiger I in Combat

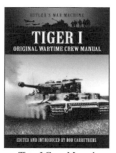
Tiger I Crew Manual

Panzers at War 1939-1942

Panzers at War 1943-1945

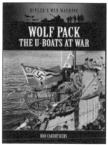
Wolf Pack - the U boats

Poland 1939

Luftwaffe Combat Reports

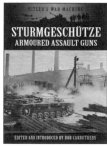
Sturmgeschütze

German Artillery in Combat

Panzer Combat Reports

The Panther V in Combat

German Tank Hunters

The Afrika Korps in Combat

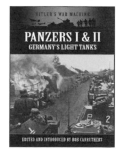
Panzers I & II

Panzer III

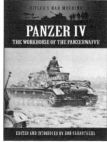
Panzer IV

For more information visit www.pen-and-sword.co.uk